D0151953

Where Peoples Meet: Racial and Ethnic Frontiers

Where Peoples

Meet

RACIAL AND ETHNIC FRONTIERS

by Everett Cherrington Hughes
and Helen MacGill Hughes

GREENWOOD PRESS, PUBLISHERS
WESTPORT, CONNECTICUT

Library of Congress Cataloging in Publication Data

Hughes, Everett Cherrington, 1897-
   Where peoples meet.

   Reprint of the ed. published by the Free Press,
Glencoe, Ill.
   Includes bibliographical references and index.
   1. Race relations. 2. United States--Race relations.
I. Hughes, Helen MacGill, 1903-   joint author.
II. Title.
[HT1521.H8 1981]   305.8'00973   80-27901
ISBN 0-313-22785-3 (lib. bdg.)

Reprinted in 1981 by Greenwood Press
A division of Congressional Information Service, Inc.
88 Post Road West, Westport, Connecticut 06881

Printed in the United States of America

10 9 8 7 6 5 4 3 2 1

Contents

Chapter One

Biases and Perspectives

In this book we discuss ideas about the contacts of peoples and the situations in which such contacts occur. Facts and ideas are to be kept together. If our observations of the contacts of people of various races and cultures are to be acute, it will be because we compare one case with another. The comparison can be made only with the aid of ideas. But the ideas will be good only in the measure that they apply to a variety of cases. We must therefore ask that you, the reader, detach yourself for the moment as far as you can from your position within your racial or ethnic group [1]

---

1. We are all members of some ethnic group just as we all are members of some race. The Oxford Dictionary defines *ethnic* as referring to "non-Israelitish," or "Gentile" nations, and ethnicism as "the religion of the Gentile nations or their common characteristics." Thus it means "people unlike ourselves," and since we are all unlike some other people, we are all ethnic. Race, on the other hand, is defined in a manner that stresses likeness. One meaning is "one of the great divisions of mankind having certain physical properties in common; a second is that it is a group connected by common descent or origin; and a third is that it is a group of people forming a distinct ethnical stock. Thus three elements enter into the notion of race: physical feature, history, and culture, three elements characteristic of all human groups. When we speak of "the race question," we usually have in mind the problems posed by the presence of someone else—not ourselves. However, whenever anyone thinks it is more diplomatic to say "human relations" instead of "race relations," he is at least admitting that the members of the other races are human.

and from the passions which go with that position; but that
you keep with you all the insight and sensitivity which you
have just because you have lived and do live your life within
such a group and in a world in which members of nearly all
groups are conscious either of strangers all about them or of
being themselves strangers. In short, keep your sensibilities
with you, but leave your prejudices behind.

This will seem an odd request, because matter concerning racial and cultural contacts is read almost exclusively
by people who pride themselves on being free of prejudices
concerning other races and cultures. Some of you readers
will have fought in the battle to reduce the disadvantages of
peoples called *minorities*. You will read these pages largely
to get new ammunition, new arguments against "discrimination," new proofs that prejudice is pathological. Perhaps
some of you will read to learn whether we who write are
on the side of the angels, or whether we hide some secret
core of prejudice which you must ferret out.

It is because we believe you, the readers, are of this kind
that we give this introduction its particular slant. If you
are, however, among those who still hold dear the unequal
distribution of privilege among racial and cultural groups
in our society and find it hard to part with the ideas which
buttress them, read these paragraphs in any case. The cause
of truth does not suffer from truth. You will find in these
pages an admission that those who suffer from prejudice
have prejudices themselves. You will be tempted to use
their prejudices to justify your own, and the actions by
which your racial, ethnic, or religious group keeps its advantages over others. Before you do it ask yourself whether you
believe the right to equality of opportunity belongs only to
those who are without fault; and especially ask where you
would be if it did. Go right ahead and read all about the
ethnocentrism of people of minority status.

It is an odd thing to say, but a true one, that many of the
people who are now studying racial and ethnic relations are
doing so from an ethnocentric point of view. This is true
sometimes in one, sometimes in both of the following senses:

they show little or no interest in the contacts of peoples outside the United States, or at most do not get beyond North America. Moreover, they look at cultural and racial relations almost entirely from the point of view of what have come to be called *minorities;* often, indeed, from the point of view of some particular minority. In this case, it may be the one to which the person himself belongs. Now, it is natural and right that the members of a disadvantaged group should fight with full force and bitterness for their rights. If they did not, our world would indeed despise them. It is also right and often good strategy for people not of a disadvantaged minority to put heart into the struggle for some one minority more than for the others, as some American white Southerners do for some American Negro Southerners. It is not the special interest in one, but the exclusion of the others from view that makes the point of view ethnocentric.

In the years since the late Professor Robert E. Park [2] directed the interest of a generation of students to this field, there has been a tremendous increase in the number of students and others interested in racial and cultural relations; but, one suspects, a decrease in the breadth of the individual student's interest: less curiosity about cultural contact as a general human phenomenon, more intense and even feverish interest in the special kinds of minority problems which are on the minds and consciences of people in

---

2. His pioneer papers are found in a single volume entitled *Race and Culture* (Glencoe: The Free Press, 1950). Park was much influenced by William I. Thomas, author, with Florian Znaniecki, of *The Polish Peasant in Europe and America* (Chicago: University of Chicago Press, 1918); and also of *Old World Traits Transplanted* (New York: Harper and Brothers, 1921)—although, for reasons which do them credit but which need not be gone into here, Park and Herbert A. Miller appear as the authors of this work. Thomas' bibliography and some of his ideas concerning the contacts of peoples appear in *Social Behavior and Personality, Contributions of W. I. Thomas to Theory and Social Research,* ed. by Edmund H. Volkart (New York: Social Science Research Council, 1951). The works of these pioneer students of cultural contacts are a fountain of ideas. Both men conceived of cultural contacts not as merely a problem to which social science should be applied, but as human phenomena from whose study social science would be developed as much as from any other.

North America and Western Europe. The Nazi persecutions forced these problems upon our attention. Many Americans, not all of them Jewish, have been affected personally or through their kin or friends by the Nazis' racial program. Others, who did not know any of the victims personally, were nevertheless filled with anxiety lest the disease spread. Some were roused either to a sense of guilt for the racial persecutions and injustices which we have passively condoned or actively supported in our own world, or to fear the vengeance which some of our own minorities of more deeply colored complexion or the awakening masses of Asia might one day visit upon the so-called white man. At any rate, the interest in racial and cultural contacts and relations has become less broad and detached, and has taken on heat and urgency. We would not reduce the heat or the sense of urgency, but we think it important that there be some people who speak from interest in all men, and from that knowledge and understanding which can come only from drawing into view a great variety of cases of contact and from seeing each not merely as a case of injustice or persecution, but as an act in the cosmic human drama. It is the duty of us of the academic world to think and speak in this mood.

From the text of some current books one might infer that the American Negro-white problem is different, not merely in detail but in kind from other racial situations; and that perhaps the oppressed of other countries somehow more nearly deserve their suffering than do American Negroes. Robert E. Park used to say that Booker T. Washington considered the Sicilian sulphur miners scarcely worthy of a better fate. They were superstitious Catholics who ate garlic. Mr. Washington passed upon them the judgment of a middle-class American Protestant; quite naturally so, for that is what he was. He had, in keeping with American tradition, risen upon a social cause. Perhaps his bias came in part from the common human tendency to consider one's own wounds and those of one's own people deeper, more painful, and less merited than those of others.

I once gave a course on the contacts of peoples to a class of French-Canadian students. In the first weeks they resisted comparison of their own position and behavior with that of other minorities. They seemed to think that comparison was an attack on the reality of their wrongs. Besides, since some other minorities were of less advanced culture, comparison with them appeared derogatory. Everyone likes to think his troubles unique. So they are, in the sense they are one's own. But an interpretation of racial and cultural relations from the point of view of a single disadvantaged group may cause members of minorities to lick their own wounds and induce functional paralysis in those morally sensitive persons who take on themselves too much of the racial guilt of their fore-bears and fellow citizens.

To help you to conceive racial and cultural contacts in a broad perspective, we have even avoided the word *minority* in the title. Why? Because the phenomenon of minority is but one of many by-products of the contacts of peoples. We will, of course, be interested in the processes by which minor-ities are made. Most of the sovereign national peoples of today have achieved their unity through a sense of being op-pressed minorities. The Norman conquest, which introduced an alien ruling class and a foreign tongue, started the inhab-itants of Great Britain on the long slow road toward nation-hood. In the time of minority status they began to become a nationality. At the end of the Great War of 1914–18, a belt of peoples lying between the empires of Western Europe and the Eastern Empire (Russia) and who had been called minor-ities by European students of politics, became nations tem-porarily. Now, in the smoldering embers of the World War which broke into the open in 1939, a larger ring of peoples (generally called "natives" by the western world to distin-guish them from the European colonial officials sent out from imperial capitals to govern them—they could scarcely be called minorities because of being so much more numer-ous than their rulers) are going through a similar cycle of believing themselves unjustly ruled by outsiders and of de-veloping a sense of nationality.

One may still ask whether the "Natives" (Negroes) of the Union of South Africa are yet a national minority. The answer lies in the extent to which these peoples, of many tribes and tongues, have come to feel themselves one in their suffering. The white man's law, by giving all Natives common disabilities and the white police, by beating them all over the head with the same club, may weld the many tribes into a single people, a minority aspiring to be a nation. We will be interested in that process wherever it occurs, and in all of its nuances—if nuance is an appropriate word for facts so rude. We study not minorities as such, but the processes and situations of contact in which peoples are made.

Interest in these processes is not new. The consequences of the contact of peoples have been a main theme of literature and history from ancient times. Herodotus is ordinarily regarded as the father of history and ethnology, for having recorded the wars and customs of the many peoples among whom a Greek-speaking traveler of the fifth century before Christ could tarry. The very fact that a man could travel so widely and yet use one language was a result of cultural contacts. From time to time one language or another has been known far beyond the borders of the country where it grew up. In Herodotus' time it was Greek. There once was an Englishman who boasted of having travelled throughout most of the world with no knowledge of any language but his own. He maintained that one could get all of his wants satisfied anywhere a train or boat would carry him by simply shouting at the top of his voice in English. Eventually someone who knew some English would be brought to pacify him and to minister to his wants. That was some years ago.

Herodotus, however, did more than record the variety of custom. He noted that some peoples were more inclined to accept outside people and outside ways than were others. He speculated upon the nature of custom as only a man can who has seen those of many peoples. Note how he proves that Cambyses, King of the Persians who then ruled over Egypt, was insane.

It is then in every way clear to me that Cambyses was outrageously mad; otherwise he would not have attempted to deride things sacred and established customs [of the Egyptians]. For if any one should propose to all men to select the best institutions of all that exist, each, after considering them all, would choose their own; so certain is it that each thinks his own institutions by far the best. It is not therefore probable that any but a madman would make such things the subject of ridicule.[3]

He noted, however, that some peoples take readily to foreign customs—the Persians being ready to adopt foreign dress, weapons and pleasures—while apparently retaining their basic familial customs.[4]

The Scythians, on the other hand, killed Anacharsis, one of their own number, buried him, and pretended that they knew nothing of him "because he travelled into Greece, and adopted foreign customs."[5]

Vico, an Italian of the 18th century, is a sort of inverted Herodotus. Interested in the old problem of making sense of the great variety of human custom, he insisted that it was necessary to study all peoples as they are, and that such study shows that even without contact with others all peoples develop certain likenesses and that all run through certain cycles of change. He accused the Greeks and Egyptians of claiming that all civilization spread from them to other people in order that they might appear as the greatest, in fact the only fully human, people on earth. They thus arrogated to themselves the credit for that common conscience of all men, which was really put in them by God.[6] Whatever may or may not be true on these matters, Vico is in the tradition of using the peoples of the earth, their varying institutions,

---

3. Herodotus. Translated by Henry Cary (London, 1877), Book III, par. 38.
4. *Op. cit.*, Book I, par. 135.
5. *Op. cit.*, Book IV, par. 76.
6. Giambattista Vico, *Die neue Wissenschaft ueber die gemeinschaftliche Natur der Voelker*. Translated into German by Erich Auerbach from the edition of 1744 of *Principi di una scienza nuova* (Principles of the new science of the common nature of the peoples). (Berlin and Leipzig: Walter De Gruyter & Co., 1930), pp. 79-80. Vico stated his principles as 113 propositions on human nature, history, politics, human origins, etc. The reference above is to Proposition 13.

and their relations to and notions about each other, as material for speculation on the nature of man and society.

Walter Bagehot, in the wake of Darwin and in the full-flowing stream of nineteenth century "progress", tried to account for that progress as a result of alternating isolation and contact. In isolation, custom and the character of a people are fixed. The cake of custom thickens and hardens until it resists change, and can be broken only by contacts and mixing. Although mixture is dangerous, since it may produce people who "have no inherited creed or plain place in the world," it is also the main source of progress, in Bagehot's view. "The problem is, why do men progress? And the answer suggested seems to be that they progress when they have a sufficient amount of variability in their nature." The variability comes, in his scheme, from the contacts of people through conquest and trade. Nationhood itself, in the modern sense, is a product of contact, of the enforced union of tribes into a larger unit. "A national character is but the successful parish character; just as the national speech is but the successful parish dialect; the dialect, that is, of the district which came to be more—in many cases but a little more —influential than other districts and so sets its yoke on books and on society." [7]

Bagehot sometimes confused a conception of social progress with biological evolution, as have other men of our time as well as of his. But his work, and that of other social theorists of the 19th century, is full of the theme of contact of peoples as a factor in human history. Gumplowicz's *Rassen-kampf* (Conflict of the Races) attributes the territorial state and law to the settling in one territory of two or more races. One becomes dominant over the other, and establishes a law which, since it applies to all within the territory, must be less personal than the tribal custom of either. The strangers, being generally conquerors, then form the top stratum in a caste or class system. As evidence, Gumplowicz cites the fact that in many parts of Europe the feudal aristocrats spoke a

---

7. Walter Bagehot, *Physics and Politics* (New York: Appleton, 1873), pp. 70, 64, 37.

tongue different from that of the local peasants and bore names of another origin. In this case, ethnic contact is offered as a determinant in the natural history of law and political institutions.

Ghurye, a leading East Indian anthropologist, accounts for the caste system in his country in similar fashion, in that he believes Indo-European conquerors excluded natives (Sudras) from their religious rituals and developed caste exclusiveness from that beginning.[8]

When scholars got around to writing the story of Christianity as documented history, the theme which seemed to turn up more than any other was that of the role of cultural contacts in creating the demand for new religions and in developing Christianity itself. In the Roman Empire a great many people were torn loose from their local gods; they seemed to want new beliefs and new faiths which would protect them even when they were far from home. A tribal god or even a city deity would not do any longer. Christianity, although based on an intensely national religion, was one of several new religions which freed themselves of territorial and ethnic limitations. The Christian god would go anywhere with you, even without an image.[9] Its main traveling missionary, Paul, was a marginal man, a Jew caught in the conflict of Jewish, Hellenistic and Roman cultures. He was, in fact, a man bred in the Pharisaic sect, which both Glover and Weber claim was a nationalistic reaction of the Jewish bourgeoisie against the pagan, immoral Greek culture under whose influence they claimed the aristocrat and the unlettered peasant had alike fallen.

These are but a few of the works of various ages which produced discussion of the contacts of races and cultures, and general hypotheses concerning their effects. They are cited here only to indicate that a great deal of social theory and of

---

8. G. S. Ghurye, *Caste and Class in India* (Bombay: The Popular Book Depot, 1950), chap. vi.

9. T. R. Glover, *The Conflict of Religions in the Early Roman Empire* (London: Methuen Co., 1909); also *Paul of Tarsus* (New York: Geo. H. Doran Co., 1925); Max Weber, *Religionssoziologie* (Tubingen: J. C. B. Mohr, 1921), Vol. III, 401, *et seq.*

the writing of history has played upon the theme of the contacts and mingling of peoples. When finally what is now called sociology began to take empirical form in England and America, its chief concern was the slum, the habitat of the new poor of the modern city. In America slum people were mostly immigrants. Books on poverty, on housing, and on the other pathologies became, in fact, books about immigrants, about the effects upon them of living in the new world, and about their influence upon America. Wars with countries from which many of our citizens and their ancestors had come, caused us concern about their loyalty. At any rate, much of American sociological work from the muckraking days of the turn of the century down to the present, has had to do with the cultural and racial contacts which have been so large a part of our national life. Thomas and Znaniecki's *Polish Peasant in Europe and America* marks the turning from an earlier journalistic to a more systematic treatment of the problems arising from immigration.

Anthropology is, for its part, not merely study of contact, but is itself, as a pursuit, cultural contact. The anthropological way of working is to go to live for a time among a strange people. Contact is the anthropologist's method; at least, it is the beginning of his method. In the interest of a fuller description of all that men have done and all the ways they have practiced, the anthropologist tries to find out what the cultures of remote peoples were like before he, the anthropologist, and other outsiders had changed them, before modern navigation and conquest had drawn nearly all of the peoples of the world temporarily into European empires. But the informants who told the anthropologist what things were like before the outsiders came, also recounted legends of more ancient migrations and contacts. It became part of the ethnological effort to seek for ever earlier and earlier connections, and to read the history of contacts from the durable fragments of articles found in ancient ruins and kitchen middens. Now that the "primitives" seem likely to be dead or on someone's payroll in fairly short order, the anthropologist has become the advocate of those whom political scientists and economists call "the backward peoples," and advisors to governments which would exploit and improve them.

Thus both sociology and anthropology are in fact sciences of the contacts of peoples, although they seek theories which will apply to all features of human society and culture.

Chapter Two

North America: Indians and Immigrants

Many books are written about the Negro problem in the United States; few, if any, about the white problem. In Canada, if one announces that he is about to study ethnic relations in Quebec, people assume that he means to study the French, not the English, Canadians. Likewise, books and articles are written about the Japanese and Chinese in America, the Flemings in France and Belgium, and the Boers in South Africa. In all of these instances, although two or more groups are in contact, one is studied rather than the other, that one which people would ordinarily call, nowadays, the minority—the immigrant, the underdog, the self-conscious group. In current studies of anti-Semitic prejudice, it is not the Jewish minority, but the Goyim, the majority, who are studied. Emphasis is still on one, rather than both, of the groups in contact.

Now there may be a certain practical logic in studying only one rather than both of a pair of peoples who live in contact with each other. The two groups generally do not know one another equally well. One may think that it is misunderstood; that it has grievances which the other group and the world outside should be made to hear. When ethnic attitudes are being studied, it is only natural that more attention should be given to the group whose opinions have more weight in the body social, economic, and politic. These practical considerations should not, however, be allowed to obscure the fact that the true unit of race and ethnic relations is not the single ethnic group, but the *situation,* embracing all of the diverse groups who live in the community or region.

Let us speak of these situations as racial or cultural frontiers, frontiers of contact.

Where are these frontiers and of what kinds are they?

Some centuries ago people of several European nationalities began to struggle with the indigenous peoples and with one another for possession of this continent. The native peoples had, of course, been in contact with one another for many centuries. American archaeologists are still digging up and putting in order the evidence of those early contacts. At the time of the invasions from overseas, the population of most of the continent north of the Rio Grande was sparser and people were less firmly attached to soil and village than in Western Europe, whence the invaders came. The Europeans traded with the natives, baptized a good many, mated with or married some of the women, killed great numbers, and pushed the remnant toward a few chronic frontiers.

Some of the native peoples, who had always taken furs for their own use, gradually devoted themselves more and more to producing furs for trade with the Europeans. They neglected the other activities by which they had produced food and the arts by which they had made houses, clothing, weapons, and tools. The more intensive trapping and hunting, combined with clearing of the forests by white men who wanted land to cultivate and wood to ship to Europe, reduced the game and pushed it back. The Indians had to go out further to hunt and trap. Their ecological base, their ties with nature and their repertory of techniques, were reduced.

Others of the native peoples were crowded and pushed in

other ways. Most of them entered into the economy of the European invaders only in its pioneering phase. As the conquerors developed a more settled agriculture and industry, they came to regard the Indians as an unmitigated nuisance. Eventually we—the acclimated descendants of the European invaders—rounded the remnants up into government-operated concentration camps whose fences, though not of barbed wire, are hardly easier to scale. The indigenous peoples of North America—at least most of them—thus became subject peoples of a peculiar sort, withdrawn from active circulation. Here and there, several developed special functions in the new economy. The Caughnawagas of the province of Quebec go about the country, even into Manhattan Island, proudly, dangerously and efficiently erecting the steel of bridges. They return, equally dangerously, in jalopies to their reservation in sight of the skyscrapers of Montreal. There they live, keeping to themselves their thoughts about the stream of summer tourists who buy their souvenirs and snap pictures of them.

Study of indigenous North Americans, the so-called Indians, has fallen to the anthropologists. The situation is that of an empire-building contact of Europeans with people of simpler technology, living in the main in small groups independent of great central political bodies. They were tribal peoples, without cities. Their history had to be reconstructed from remains other than dated documents. Anthropologists go after such peoples, generally leaving those with richly documented pasts to historians, and those of contemporary Western culture to sociologists, economists and political scientists. American anthropology grew up on the native cultures of America, reconstructing past migrations and contacts, piecing together what things used to be like from material remains and from long-lived informants with still longer memories.

The role of special students of Indian cultures led the anthropologists naturally to become the special guardians and champions of living Indians. And the Indians have plenty of grievances to keep their advocates busy. Tuberculosis, poor diet, illiteracy (for the Indian who can't read is no longer preliterate, but illiterate), racial discrimination on the streets, in industry, the army, and the cemetery, these make the Indians a social problem, in the same sense that the slum-dwelling European immigrant—who belonged to the sociologists—was a problem in his green-horn days. The resurgent, restless Indians of today are demanding admission without discrimination into the main economy of the country and also insisting on their right to maintain and even restore their native social order and economy on what they consider their own land. They are thus becoming a true charter-member minority in spirit, as well as by virtue of their history.

The people of European origin drove off the natives that they themselves might exploit the land. Exploit it they did, with fury and fervor. In some regions the Indians sitting on their reservations have seen two or three distinct breeds of exploiters sweep over the land, each with its own mode of exploitation. In most regions, geographers say, the present inhabitants are still using up resources of soil and water, not yet having disciplined themselves to a land use that can long endure. The exploitation of America is still in the experimental stage.

So far it has been a series of ethnic experiments. Each of the earlier groups of settlers surveyed, occupied, and used the land in its own peculiar ways, adapting them in some measure to the region. Eventually the settlements of one European group met those of another, making a new set of ethnic frontiers. The now old frontier between French-Canadians and New Englanders is still active on both rural and urban fronts in both Canada and the United States.

Dutch and English met early in New York. The Germans got into Pennsylvania and New York long before the Revolutionary War, and the cultural frontier between them and other settlers was politically active for a long time; it is still demographically active. The French and Spanish people of the Gulf Coast settlements, a varied lot, were eventually overwhelmed by English-speaking Americans, white and black.

The Spanish and the Anglos met and clashed in Texas and throughout what are now, as a result of the conflict, our southwestern states. Each of these frontiers has been, at one time or other, a frontier of land use, economy, and social structure as well as of language, religion, and political allegiance.

While these older frontiers were still in flux, new ones were being created by continued migration from various European countries. The variety was made greater by the fact that many of the settlers came with not merely a national or regional culture, but with some new religious faith. They were determined to establish the true kingdom of God on some isolated, but fertile, American site. If their new inspiration had not yet settled into a culture by the time of their arrival, it soon did so here, although the process was complicated by the swarming off of dissenting groups to found still newer heavens. Sects, although they may claim to be interested only in the next world, have often developed into highly inbred, exclusive, and rigidly traditional societies in this world; [1] in short, into ethnic groups. Sects, living in their own communities, tend—said Robert E. Park—to become tribes. In North America they have often become prosperous tribes. There are still many of them, each with its active, defensive frontier of contact with the world. In our colleges, and especially in the teachers' colleges of the midwest, are thousands of students still caught in the struggle of sectarian community and family with the ways of the outside world.

In due time political boundaries grew fixed. The United States and Canada became the two great North American empires. Like other empires, they included people of many nations, languages, religions, and races. Unlike other empires, their territories were all in one piece, not divided by seas. The reduction of the political sovereignties of the con-

---

1. Charles Nordhoff, *The Communistic Societies of the United States from Personal Visit and Observation* (London: J. Murray, 1875); Ellsworth Faris, "The Sect and the Sectarian," *The Nature of Human Nature* (New York: McGraw-Hill Book Co., 1937).

tinent to two, both dominated by people of English language and British institutions, made historic minorities of the other peoples who lived in them. For the term "minority" was historically applied in Europe to a group of people living on a soil which they have occupied from time immemorial, but who, through change of boundaries, have become politically subordinate. They are strangers, though at home. These we may call "charter-member" minorities.

The French are the charter-member minority in Eastern Canada. The lay-out of fields, the arrangement of houses in the country and in villages, the architecture and structure of towns and cities, the very landscape, proclaim to the eye that this region was not settled by the same people as New England and neighboring Ontario. The French named the rivers and the towns. Folklore, antiques in roadside shops, all that relates to the past, is French. In Louisiana it was likewise French people who made their mark upon the landscape, tradition, and even the law. In parts of the Southwestern states it was Spanish-speaking Mexicans.

In these regions the Roman Catholic church is not, as in most parts of the country, the church of later immigrants who came as laborers, but the church of the charter-member minority, including the remnants of an aristocracy as well as many unskilled workers of the same ethnic background. The charter-member Latin Catholics of these regions struggle—generally in vain—to keep control of the church from the more aggressive "American" Catholics of Irish and German background.[2] Within the bosom of the Catholic church, there are ethnic patterns of practice. Each ethnic group has its favorite festivals and saints. So different are the patterns that a visiting Brazilian student remarked that a high mass

2. Recently a study was made of the practice of the faith by Catholics of various social and economic position in the diocese of St. Augustine. Spanish-Americans, who are the charter-member Catholics there and are, in fact, the majority of all Catholics, were left out of the study. The Catholics of "English" culture alone were considered—northern Irish and German Catholics who came down for the winter, and stayed on.—Cf. George A. Kelley, *Catholics and the Practice of the Faith.* (Washington, D. C.: Catholic University of America Press, 1946.)

in Chicago resembles the morning service of a Presbyterian
Church more than the Catholic service in Brazil. The people here sit down in their pews, listen to a sermon, and don't
leave until all is over—the Latin practice is that of individual
devotion, prayers at a side altar or in front of a favorite saint,
with constant coming and going and nothing much done in
concert. Several patterns of Catholicism are in contact, and
sometimes in conflict, in North America. Among American
Catholics, the French and the Spanish are the charter-member minorities.

Other historic charter-member minorities are the people
of German and Swiss ancestry who gave their character to
parts of Pennsylvania, New York, Maryland, and Virginia,
and some of whom fought to make public bodies in those
regions bilingual. Less historic, in that they came later and
are less well-recorded in the history books, are the many
regions further west originally settled by other than English-
speaking people. In Texas is a large region whose first settlers were Germans who expected to found there a German
state. In other western states, Germans, Bohemians, Scan-
dinavians—although often preceded by Yankee pioneers—
were the people who really filled up the country and culti-
vated it. Swedish and Norwegian historical societies are still
collecting documents on the role of their people in the settlement of the Northwest. The areas so settled vary from
small communities to large regions.

Among the charter-member groups are some which have
been called "cultural islands"—small communities of people
hanging on to a peculiar culture, heedless of the march of
modern America. There are little pockets of Amish people
who, bearded and in plain dress, drive in their horse-drawn
buggies to city markets to sell the produce of their prosperous farms. One senses that their prosperity is part of their
protection against the world. In other cases it seems that poverty is the cultural preservative, as with the backwoods,
bayou fishing and fur-trapping communities of French
speech in Louisiana. It has not yet been worth while for the
big world to ferret them out. In some mountain districts peo-

ple of purest Anglo-Saxon origin constitute little pockets maintaining early American adaptations of English folk-song and tale, and an archaic speech. In the South are many small, purposely isolated, racial and cultural communities consisting each of a few families produced by some mixture of Negro with English, Spanish, French, Indian, or other ancestry. The people of these little islands cling fanatically to French culture, or to any other symbol by which they may keep themselves from being absorbed into the category and status of Negro, to which we North Americans try to relegate all people suspected of some other than European ancestry. Going to high school in a county town, asking for relief or for a government crop loan, entering the army, or seeking a job in a factory with a personnel department—all these steps, or any other which lead to making out a paper about one's self, they avoid. For where there is a paper, there is racial classification: one becomes fatally and fully Negro, unless he can "pass" and become anxiously white. The discovery of some resource attractive to industry on their doubtfully held lands, some ultimate poverty or some vision of the outside world which makes their youth seek, if not fortune, at least glamor and a better living in cities—these are the breaches that let the big world pour in.

There are still many such pockets not yet swept out by the broom of our industrial and urban civilization. The sectarian communities were generally settled by people so fanatical as to believe that, since men are equal before God, they should be so before one another. Some sects tried common holdings of land and goods. But in most, in spite of equalitarian sentiment, a few families became wealthier and more powerful than others. Such families have property and position within the small community to pass on to their children. They can give substantial rewards to those who, though tempted by the world, remain faithful. The young Mennonite who is shunned for defiantly following too much some way of the world may lose more than the fellowship of his family and neighbors; and the world probably offers him little in return for his pains. Perhaps it is better to be respected and prosperous in plain dress and a buggy than to be in the great world, a barehanded worker in industry, driven by guilt to be a rate-buster and a chronic "outsider."

We don't yet know what makes cultural pockets survive. Perhaps prosperity helps the divergent sect because it gives the members something to offer their children. A certain measure of poverty may help those who remain apart to keep from falling into the Negro caste. The combinations of outward circumstance with inward motivation operating in such cases still want working out.

Whenever our economy has needed labor and couldn't get it from overseas, it has drawn upon the pool of native labor in these cultural and racial pockets. How long it will take to mop them up no one knows. The process seems to be going on rapidly now, but it will probably last longer than any of us would predict.

When people speak of a farm in North America they generally refer to an enterprise in which members of the family work the land with, perhaps, now and then some hired labor. Much of the land has been and is worked in this way. But there are exceptions, and each has created its special pattern of racial or ethnic relations. The great early exception was in the Southern colonies where—although there were and are many family farmsteads, a large-scale and highly commercial agriculture developed from the beginning of settlement. Here were the plantations.

The labor to produce the large commercial crops was brought from abroad at the expense of the employer, the plantation owner. This is a common enough phenomenon. Many poverty-stricken Europeans let their way hither be paid by American settlers in return for some years of service after arrival. Industries have often sent agents abroad to recruit labor and pay its passage; labor contractors of various ethnic groups have transported their countrymen—on commission—to places where labor is wanted. In this country immigrants already here have sent home savings to pay the way of kinsmen and future brides. What turned out to be different in the Southern states was that the immigrants—Africans of Negro race—were forced to come and were not parties to the contract at all. Ship-owners—some of them pious New England Puritans—bought the Negroes from captors, carried them across the Atlantic, and sold them to traders and plantation-owners. In time the institution of chattel slavery developed; these persons could be and were bought and sold. They ceased to have a claim on the price of their labor, and so could not buy their freedom by working off the cost of their unwilling passage from Africa.

The Africans were transported not as kin, tribal, or village groups, but as individuals. They were put to work in groups which had no relation to their previous forms of organization. They were brought forcibly and quickly into contact with certain features of the developing culture of the American South. From other aspects of Southern life they were strictly isolated. It was made against the law in some states for the slaves to be taught to read or to learn skilled trades. But the plantation racial frontier was a domestic—literally, a household—one. What intimate services slaves and masters performed for one another, and what they learned from each other could not be completely controlled by law.

Some say that the Africans in North America have kept little of their African cultures and social forms. Others say they have kept much. The controversy over the point is conducted with some heat.[3] Perhaps sociologists would like to make the evil done the African in America greater by showing that he was stripped of his culture as well as of his freedom. The anthropologist may want to pay him the compliment of showing that he kept some of his culture in spite of all. Since the contacts of peoples so often raise arguments concerning justice in which facts of the history of culture are invoked, one may expect conflicts over such points. This

---

3. E. Franklin Frazier, *The Negro in the United States* (New York: Macmillan, 1949); Melville Herskovitz, *The Myth of the Negro Past* (New York: Harper's, 1941).

is but one case, and an unusual one because in it both sides agree as to who is the victim of injustice.

The Africans differed from other immigrants to North America in that they could be distinguished and defined not merely by cultural behavior—such as language, clothing, food and religion—but by racial features as well.

In time they came to be called, not by cultural features, place of origin, nor by any name they had ever had for themselves, but by their color as seen by Europeans. The Europeans called all Africans—brown, black, and purple—by names meaning black; by contrast, the rather iridescent, often ruddy, sometimes yellowish, greenish, or brownish European became a white man. Color names thus became the most important of social tags in North America.

The forced migration of Africans by which the highly commerical agriculture of the South got its labor force gave us our most fateful racial frontier and a running series of social problems, some chronic, some lurking dormant to become acute whenever some crisis arises. The manufacturing states of New England come into conflict with the raw-material producing South! Negro slavery becomes part of the issue. A manpower shortage! Shall we use Negro labor? A war! Migrations! Housing shortages! Always there is the Negro angle, for we are—next to the whites of South Africa —probably the most race-conscious people the world has ever known. Few are the situations which both Negro and white Americans enter, side by side, unlabeled and undifferentiated. Even a monk or a hero must be named by his color, unless he is white. The Nazis may have outdone us in elaboration of racial law, in the thoroughness of their discrimination, and certainly in the fanatical determination to extirpate what they called the races of less worth. But the Germans have never approached us in the finesse of racial etiquette, and in the sensitivity of the eye to any sign of color or racial feature. As the Nazis reached the pinnacle of formal and determined racial policy, we have approached the limit of informal sensitivity, attention and social control.

When Asiatics later entered the labor force on the west coast of North America, adding new variety to our racial composition, we were already accustomed to call people by color names, and had at hand a pattern of racial discrimination to apply to them. But the Asiatic immigrants did not come as slaves, and although, like the Negro, they were excluded from skilled trades and from manufacturing industries, they soon succeeded in becoming independent small traders and farmers. They did not so willingly accept color definition, perhaps because they are light skinned, perhaps because they soon learned that in North America a color name is not merely a tag but an epithet.

From the very beginning there were Negroes who either with or without help from white men got away to new places and to a new station. Black and white mixed so that the name Negro became more and more a social tag, less and less a description. Then, as cities and industries grew, and labor became short, Negroes began to move to the cities and to seek places in industry, or were wooed by strike-ridden or man-hungry employers.

The frontiers mentioned thus far, including the Negro-white one in the South, were rural in their beginnings and continued so in large measure. But Americans early established manufacturing industries. They wanted labor. It was supplied by a long and immense stream of migrants across the Atlantic; first, from near the eastern shores of the ocean. Eventually, the draw was so great as to suck people from the very heart of Europe. The European immigrant to American cities and industrial centers became the prime object of study of the American empirical sociologist, who was at first scarcely distinguishable from the muck-raking journalist and the then emerging social worker. In England, at the end of the 19th century, Charles Booth and his associates covered most of London on foot to inquire into the manner of life of the new urban and industrial masses. They classified the people according to the trades they worked at, believing this the most significant clue to differences in condition of

life.[4] In North America of the same epoch the social sur-
veyors found that to describe the city slum was, in fact, to
describe the little Irelands, Polands, Sicilies, and the Ghettoes. Indeed, they learned that the block a man lived in and
the saloon he drank in might depend even upon the county
of Ireland in which he had been born, and that the Jew wor-
shipped with *Landsmaenner* of his own province or even
village in Roumania. To tell the horror of a coal mining
camp or of a smoky hillside in a steel town required the social surveyor to tell about the Welshmen or Slavs who lived
there. In London the settlement house was a device for
workers' education; here it became an Americanization
agency. The American reformer, social surveyor, and sociologist set out to study the slum; he became, in so doing, a student of the accommodation to the American economy and
of the assimilation to American society of the European
peasant who became, by a single sea-change, a city-dweller
and a laborer in construction or manufacturing.

Some of these investigators, notably W. I. Thomas and
Robert E. Park,[5] saw in these processes called "Americanization" merely one case of the eternal interaction of men with
each other and with their environments. This may account
for a difference in the sociological and anthropological vo-
cabularies concerning contacts of people and cultures. The
anthropologist was, for a long time, mainly interested in the
culture, rather than the people, and so talked about what
happens to cultural traits. Acculturation, diffusion, culture
areas referred, originally, not to people at all (although there
is now talk of "acculturated individuals"). The sociological
words (competition, conflict, accommodation, assimilation—
taken from Georg Simmel's theory of social interaction) referred rather to the experiences and behavior of people. As

4. Charles Booth, *Life and Labour of the People of London* (London:
1889–91).
5. W. I. Thomas and Florian Znaniecki, *The Polish Peasant in Europe
and America* (Chicago: University of Chicago Press, 1918); and Robert E.
Park, *Race and Culture* (Glencoe, Ill.: The Free Press, 1950); also Park and
Herbert A. Miller, *Old World Traits Transplanted* (New York: Harper and
Bros., 1921).

the two kinds of study have approached each other, the two terminologies have half-blended in a grand confusion.

In due time the rural Negro American became an immigrant to the industrial cities of the North. When he did so he started to run through much of the cycle of experience of the European immigrant; living in the slum ghettoes, starting at the bottom of the industrial hierarchy, quarrelling with his urban-bred children. A similar thing happened to the Negro's *Landsmann,* the rural white Southerner who also came north for a job. The latter's case has been different from that of the European immigrant, however, in that both the Negro and white American from the South consider themselves as charter members of this country and in the Northern city find themselves working for bosses whom they regard as foreigners.

Study of the Negro-white frontier has been going on for a long time, but it was given new impetus by the movement of Negroes into industrial cities where they became a "social problem," and also by the rise of a Negro middle class who could carry on these studies as part of their struggle for a new status. At any rate, study of Negro-white relations has joined and, in some measure, superseded study of immigrants as a main interest of American sociologists.

Chapter Three

The Peoples Meet Everywhere

In most of the many West Indian Islands, as in our plantation states, Europeans imported Africans to do the labor of producing a few staples for the world market. Here and there a remnant of the indigenous population survived either through admixture with the imported labor or retreat into regions not suited to the new cultivation. The original composition and later mixture of races varied and still varies from island to island, according as the European masters were British, Spanish, French or Dutch (sometimes one succeeded another), according to the kinds and numbers of African, East Indian and other laborers imported and according to various geographic, economic, and political contingencies.

But the variations do not drown out the common theme. A top class of people of European ancestry owned and managed the plantations and all related enterprises. In the earlier days they also owned the laborers; after formal emancipation they continued as before to govern the islands without interference from the laborers. The people of the top class were few in number relative to the laboring class or caste (as it came to be in some cases) of non-Europeans. Between the two main classes was a great emptiness, a status gap. The one class lived in the grand style, albeit in some islands the grandeur became pathetic and bedraggled. The others lived in misery, albeit often a colorful, tropical misery attractive to tourists. Of people in between, so numerous and important in North America, there were none at first.

Such a status gap may be filled by people falling from the top for want of property or an economic place proper to their high social position. It may be filled by people who climb from the bottom. When these two things happen in the West Indies people of more European ancestry, hence lighter in color, enter into more nearly equal competition with people of less European ancestry, hence darker, who have come up from the bottom. This is generally considered a political and social crisis by those on top. They prevent it if they can by measures which vary from island to island.

In all of the islands the classes, hence the races, interbred. In those islands where the top class was and is British, they draw a race line and attempt to keep themselves free of any African taint. In those where the masters were of the Latin countries, the race line was not made into a caste line. The upper classes are merely lighter in color than the lower, as in the Haitian republic.

But the presence or absence of a strict race line gives no clue to the class composition, relative standards of living and possibilities of social and economic climbing on an island. In some island societies which draw no race line it is almost impossible for a person of the agricultural or urban laboring masses or of the poverty-stricken peasant classes to rise. Such is the case in both Haiti and Puerto Rico, both of which have no race line, but both of which do have poverty-stricken masses which supply labor to other islands and to the continental United States.

The French-speaking middle and upper class families of Haiti are light-skinned mulattoes. When their diplomatic representatives travel in the United States the State Department surrounds them with escorts to save them from racial insults by us, the American people. Yet at home they are reported to oppose all measures that would make it easy for the black peasant to rise. The republic has two languages, French and a patois known as *creole*. All classes speak creole. Only the middle and upper classes speak French. By conducting all public affairs in French and by discouraging the common people from learning French, those on top keep a monopoly of many positions, including that of translator in courts and other public offices.[1] A language and literacy barrier limits competition from the lower classes just as a race line may do elsewhere. On the other hand, in some of the British islands, where there is still a "pure white" owning class, the bulk of the professional people and civil servants may be colored, that is, mixed Negro and European. A colored man may sit in judgment over white men in a court or give medical treatment to their wives. In general, West Indian poor people are numerous and very poor indeed; and they are darker of skin than people who are not poor. The sharpness of the color line, and its location on the social status scale vary from island to island. These things, however, will not tell one anything about the measure of poverty or of the individual's chances of improving his lot on a given island.

The old top class in the islands was based on land. But there isn't much land, and its amount is fixed. If the members of the top class increased in number at all—and they did —there were too many of them. The descendants of the great owners have provided for one another as best they can by trying to keep for themselves all positions of prestige and good income.[2] Hence the tenacity with which the Haitian middle class hangs on to its monopoly of education. The struggle of the old middle and upper classes is not to fall in the scale of wealth and position; if they are white, it is the struggle not to become that despised misfit, the poor white.

---

1. This information was given us by Dr. Price-Mars, a Haitian scholar and diplomat, about ten years ago. We are not sure about the present situation. Our aim, in any case, is to present the kinds of things people do, not the latest news.

2. Eric Williams, *The Negro in the Caribbean* (Washington, D. C., 1942).

Many people of the formerly wealthy classes have emigrated. Their remittances are in some islands an important part of the income of those who remain at home.

Recently entrepreneurs of a new style have appeared in some of the islands, either to exploit a resource not previously so important, or to reorganize what is already in operation. The new enterprises may not want the skills of the old middle and upper classes. The new men with North American color and cultural prejudices may see little distinction between educated "gentlemen" and illiterate labor, if both have darkish skins and speak a strange tongue; they may perceive no difference between that which is stereotyped in "You come on-a my house, my husban' don' mind," and the close and jealous guarding of women in the middle-class Latin family.

The old middle and upper classes, already distressed by lack of economic elbow-room, find their position undermined by a new and foreign economy, and their culture and social leadership either ignored or contemptuously attacked. They are thus made into charter-member minorities, and may turn into what we of the continental United States, with completely unconscious irony, call "nationalists" in the case of Puerto Rico.

Meanwhile, the press of agricultural laborers and of independent peasants—where there are such—upon the land becomes acute. Agrarian restlessness combines with labor unrest in the towns and seaports. It is slightly, but only slightly, relieved by immigration to the continental United States, where our labor force is so short that we have relaxed the old rule against contract labor, and are importing colored hands again. Airplanes ply back and forth carrying these newest immigrants to their jobs and then back home to exhibit their glamor. With them go the rumors and dreams which stir very poor people whenever any of them start moving out into the big world. Every poor boy in the Puerto Rican cities is becoming a future—no, not President of the United States—but champion featherweight boxer, and his dancing partner a future night club entertainer, even a Hollywood star.

These islands present an almost infinite variety. Some are as they were; in others change is going on at revolutionary rate. Each is the scene of some variation of the drama which arises through change in relative number of the classes. Bermuda is encouraging its colored population to practice birth control, because there are so many of them that the white people can't afford to hire them all as servants and gardeners. A large part of the white population of each generation migrates from Barbados as Negroes rise to compete for the few middle-class positions. Jamaica has a labor movement, tied with racial unrest; it has long had mulatto squatters who ran from their owners in the days of slavery and settled in the mountains to become free peasants. Population and change are catching up with them, too. Every one of the islands, although isolated physically and biologically, has its own measure of sensitivity to the demographic, economic, political, and cultural events of the outside world. On every one of them are active racial and/or cultural frontiers.

In most of North America, the indigenous peoples were so completely driven off that the main racial and ethnic frontiers are those between peoples of the various European countries. In the South and the West Indies, importation of African labor made the contact of white upper class with a Negro laboring class the great racial frontier. In parts of Central and South America is a third situation. The indigenous peoples occupied parts of the land densely and were held to it by an intensive agriculture, by permanent villages and even by cities. In spite of much slaughter and dislocation by the invaders, many of the indigenous people remained in their home territory and grew some of the same crops as before. The invaders became their masters. It is almost a classical case of the kind to which Gumplowicz attributes the stratification of societies: a numerous people attached to the soil becomes subordinate to a few invaders of another ethnic group who form a ruling class.

The indigenous peoples, again of darker skin than their masters, became in effect forced labor for commercial agriculture. Unlike the forced labor of our Southern states, they were near home and could preserve much of their culture and social organization. They became a cross between a less-than-free laboring class and a charter-member minority, preserving their arts, language and social forms against invading foreign masters. As in other parts of the world where invaders succeeded in using a native labor force in a new economy, many of the social units were indeed broken up and the society was organized along new lines in course of time. The newcomers brought a system of land ownership that violated native custom. Whole areas were put under a single crop until the soil was exhausted or the world demand for it petered out. There were insurrections which temporarily drove the Europeans out of an area here and there. Sometimes the jungle grew up again, and people of primitive economy moved in to live by their traditional means plus a sewing machine and some folk Catholicism. The Spanish language and culture and the Catholic religion were planted in the cities and in spots on the countryside; they spread out slowly, more or less diluted, into more remote parts.

Tribes of indigenous culture and speech, peasants more or less Spanish of culture, laborers of the plantations, of the mines, of town and city industries, all are citizens of Mexico, Guatemala, or Colombia. Not all of them know it. And that is part of the cultural frontier, too. For in these countries the important thing about a man seems to be not whether his physical features are those of an Indian rather than of a European white man, but whether he lives in a little village or tribal world with its own gods and speech, or in the big world that leads out to cities where politics and business are carried on. In Latin America one can see in their various phases the processes by which politically conscious peoples are made.

Thus in times past, while there were many tribes and peoples in Mexico, there was no Mexican people. There is one now, and it embraces more and more of the population.

Sometimes the rise of a new political people takes the form of a cultural revival. In Mexico, this has been the Indian revival. Artists of the Mexican revolution have filled their canvasses and covered the walls of public buildings with figures which are Indian in feature and costume. The Indian symbolizes not merely the past, but the suffering of the common people of the present and their victory over reaction in the future. The future will belong to the people; the people are Indian. In the cultural revival that which was despised by the invader and was neglected by the people themselves is brought back to life as part of a movement to stir them all to action to improve their present state. The symbols of the past become the symbols of a common future. Often a cultural revival includes an attempt to restore a language, as was the case in Ireland. In Mexico this is not so. None of the numerous indigenous tongues is sufficiently widespread to be a candidate for the national language. The language of the Mexican political people will apparently be that of the Spanish invaders.

The racial and cultural frontiers of some of the other Central American and South American countries are like the Mexican, in that the Spanish or Portuguese invaders eventually established large scale agriculture or mining with the aid of indigenous or African labor. But we would be deceived if we think of Latin America in stereotypes. The variety of situation is great. There are native tribes, among the most primitive in the world in their way of living and only slightly touched by European civilization. In the high Andes people with much of the Inca culture live in villages and towns that are among the oldest in this hemisphere; some of them are now being disturbed by American corporations which establish mines and industries in their region and set before them another way of life in company towns built to attract and keep native labor. In much of Brazil a plantation system was built on African slave labor. But there, unlike North America, Africans continued to come of their own will. Brazilian Negroes have developed a culture quite different from that of North American Negroes. Moreover,

Brazil and the Argentine have received successive waves of European immigrants right down to the present. In Brazil, many Germans of pietistic sects have founded villages of homesteading farms. Japanese peasants have settled in a similar fashion, developing profitable small family farms on land that the plantation economy had either worn out or not used at all. The cities of Brazil are, like our own, of fascinating ethnic and racial complexity.

James Bryce, after a grand tour, compared the relations of the races in South America with those in North America and other places where Europeans had conquered the "backward" races. "The distinction between the races," he said, "is in South America a distinction of rank or class rather than of colour." [3] To many North Americans Brazil especially has become the shining example of a country with great racial variety but with no color line. Brazilian students who come to this country to study are expected to go about publicly and conspicuously playing the role of people without prejudice. It must be said that except in this symbolic way, North American students of racial contacts have made little use of Brazil and other South American countries. And this use, laudable as it may be, stereotypes the local racial situation. It is apparently true that Brazil is remarkably free of racial prejudice. In fact, a Brazilian reports that a Sao Paulo rabbi has complained that there is so little anti-Semitism there that it is difficult to keep his synagogue alive. On the other hand, a Brazilian student tells of a Negro physician, prominent in his small town and married to a woman of high social standing, who—in the metropolis of Sao Paulo —was waiting for a cab at a public stand. A white man, taking him for the cab starter, handed him a large tip and asked him to hold the next cab for him. Where personal acquaintance gives way to anonymity, color is apparently the badge of lower status. The man who gave the tip would, of course, have sat down gladly at table with the other in the proper

---

3. *South America, Observations and Impressions* (New York: Macmillan, 1912), chap. xiii, "The Relations of Races in South America," cf. p. 471, *et passim*.

circumstances. Many a Negro United States American has been pained to find that Brazil does not receive him with open arms. As in most of the Latin American countries, class and family distinctions are great and are maintained by social exclusiveness. The exclusiveness may cut white and Negro more or less alike, but it hurts the North American Negro more.

Our knowledge of how men act on racial cultural frontiers cannot approach completeness without analyzing the rich and varied situations of Latin America. Do Italian vinegrowers in the Argentine become assimilated in the same way and at the same rate as in California? Do German sectarians and Japanese peasants run the same course of adjustment as in North America? Is it something about North American Gentiles, or something about European Jews, that makes them form ghettoes here more than in South American cities? These and a thousand other questions arise as one looks in that direction.

Europe is the home of the modern nation-state and of the most determined struggles to make it a reality in old settled country. The concept is that of a nation (a people) who recognize themselves as one, living alone in a clearly-bounded territory where a government which they identify as their own keeps the peace within and represents them without. The essence of the idea of nation is that of a people who recognize themselves as one. Generally, in fact, such a people is of one race and one culture and has at least the fiction of a common past, even of common biological ancestry. Since nationhood implies pious loyalty, it is not astonishing that a religion is sometimes part of the common culture. Sometimes national sentiment has been strong enough to outweigh religious diversity, sometimes not. The irreducible essence of the idea of the state is monopoly of police power within a territory. In the concept of nation-state the two, nation and state, concide. As historical reality, they never quite do so.

But back of this concept lies the historic development of

peoples themselves. Reconstruction of the basic migrations and consequent mixtures of breed and culture which created the European peoples of today has been a major preoccupation of historians. They lie well in the past. But one must remember that every people, no matter how old in fact and in fiction, is an historical entity. Some of the languages of Europe were once the vernaculars of cultural frontiers; before purity comes mixture. The customs, institutions, and laws of the peoples of Europe were products of the contact of the expanding Graeco-Roman, eventually Christian, civilization with native cultures, and of these with one another. The great Islamic world was long a contender for the Mediterranean margins of Europe, and also made its contributions to the European cultures. These things we say, not to inform, but to remind students of cultural contacts that back of the concept of the nation-state lies the long historic evolution of peoples themselves out of the dialectic between contact and isolation.

When nation-states did develop they were always short of the ideal. Ethnic boundaries turned out to be broad belts, not thin lines such as customs officers can supervise. A few villages of Wendish peasants remain enclaved in Prussian swamps centuries after the German invaders have settled around them. A few German-speaking peasants swarm off to live on the boundaries of Hungary and Roumania; others seek religious refuge in far-off Russian plains, and build and maintain a culture there. A diaspora of South German Catholics is scattered in little colonies in Baltic cities, feeling alien and considered alien by the Protestant Germans about them. Some peoples with a long history and considerable territory either never achieved nation-statehood or lost it. Friesians, Flemings, Poles, Czechs, Irish, Welsh, Scottish, Basques, all these are names of peoples with territory language, customs, and some sense of group identity. Some have had states and lost them. Some live under one, others are divided among several sovereignties which think of themselves as nation-states. These various territorially based ethnic peoples press against one another for space with their varying rates of increase of population and their varying ways of cultivating land and exploiting resources as the competitive weapons. From time to time military weapons intervene in the process and the boundaries are changed. Sometimes the new boundary fits ethnic lines better than the old; sometimes not.

The great labor migrations of the nineteenth century further confused the reality. No great industrial region of Europe has a labor force of a single ethnic or national stock. Poles came in huge numbers to man the mines and heavy industries of the German Rhineland. Heavy industry in the North of England and Scotland drew people from the South and from Ireland. In eastern Germany, Poland, and to some extent in Bohemia, it was management which was strange. This made new urban enclaves of ethnic strangers in the national body.

In the period before the first World War, the ethnic minorities of Europe were stirring. Half-forgotten folk-lore was revived as a symbol of the antiquity of the culture of one's people. Groups of ardent young nationalists turned their backs on the languages of empire (German, Russian) and wrote poems and tracts in Polish, Czech, Ukrainian, or some other "minority" language.[4] The would-be international and socialist movements were plagued by resurgent ethnic consciousness among the workers. At the end of the war new nation-states were created and boundaries of old ones adjusted. There were to be no more empires in Europe. The nation-state was to come into its own.

Still the ethnic realities did not fit territorial reality and conflicting claims. Eventually the National-Socialists, declaring Germany again an empire, rather than a republic, resorted to drastic methods. They set up a sharply exclusive definition of what is ethnically German, and purged, drove out, or reduced to subordinate status those who did not fit it. At the same time they set up an inclusive definition in trying to restore the older conception that all people of true

---

4. The role of language in these nationalist movements is described in Robert E. Park, *The Immigrant Press and Its Control* (New York: Harper and Bros., 1922), chap. ii.

German descent belonged to the German people and owed loyalty to the German state, and in claiming as their own whatever territory might be required to allow all true Germans to live contiguously and at what they considered their rightful standard of living. This program was called "realistic" by the Nazis, presumably because it appeared the only way to bring to drastic, logical and ultimate realization the unquestioned doctrine of the nation-state. It might have been more realistic to recognize that, if there is to be more than one nation-state in the world, and since there will probably be more than one, none of them will ever correspond completely to the concept.

The end is not yet of violent methods to square ethnic and loyalty boundaries with those of political powers. The pause in the wars in 1944 and 1945 has been followed by new shifting of boundaries and by huge new migrations. Some of the migrations are forced, and the Germans have invented the new word *"Ausgewiesene"* to distinguish those who have been shown the gate from the refugees, or *Fluechtlinge,* who fly for their liberty or lives. They helped, too, to create the displaced person, although we are not sure they bothered to name that phenomenon. In the Europe of today there are new frontiers of mass contact; there are also new iron curtains to isolate even people of the same nation and language from each other. Whether ideologies will permanently be more powerful than national sentiment in uniting and dividing people, we do not venture to say. At the moment the situation is so confused that minority—as a term to designate some poor people whose homeland is temporarily under foreign rule—sounds a simple and rather old-fashioned term.

The name Middle East has lately been applied to a belt extending from Morocco on the west, across that part of Africa which faces the Mediterranean, through Egypt, the Arabian peninsula, the eastern shore of the Mediterranean, and on through Mesopotamia and Persia (Iraq and Iran) to the hither borders of India and Pakistan. This is the territory of the Islamic world, in which the new Israel is encysted. Archaeologists dig at various places in it for evidence of the early contacts by which were spread the cultivation of grains, domestication of animals, use of metals and of the wheel, and many other arts so important to the rise of cities and empires. The diggings have been financed and directed by Europeans; the shovels have been wielded by natives of the region, probably descendants of the ancient peoples whose history lies buried there. The archaeology itself was a product of cultural contact, and of the empire-building which put all of this belt for a time under the dominion of Europeans.

In this cradle of civilizations and religions, militant Islam arose and served as the great integrator as did Christianity in Europe. It began, like Christianity, in cities. It travelled with the caravan to the desert and mountain frontiers where tribesmen became Muslims in name while retaining many of their old practices. Like Christianity, Islam has had its dissenting leaders, its revivals, and sectarian schisms. It is still full of sects, new and old, backwoodsy and cosmopolitan, illiterate and learned, wildly ecstatic and quietly contemplative. Muslim has fought Muslim over matters of succession to religious and political office, and over matters of faith. Empires have spread and long held sway over large parts of the area. Always there have been pilgrimages to holy cities, which have brought ethnic strangers into contact with one another. There have been periods of intellectual activity when were established universities, libraries and orders of learned brothers in the faith.

The cities of the Middle East generally retain an ethnic division of labor. The people of a given origin, or of a certain religion or Islamic sect, do a certain kind of work from generation to generation. They also live in their own quarter, and under the law of their own kind. This stands in sharp contrast to the present tendency of the western world, where—although various ethnic groups may be concentrated in certain trades or in certain positions in industry—everyone is considered a potential candidate for any trade or job and lives under a law that applies to all in the territory. The

Middle Eastern world offers the spectacle of people retaining their cultural differences in spite of living in close proximity and in economic interdependence for centuries.

At the present time this whole belt is in the world news. Iran is in conflict with Britain over control of oil; Egypt, over control of Suez. The Moroccans and Tunisians demand freedom from French control. Israel is at odds with the surrounding Arab world which considers this new state the latest European colony in its midst, a colony which is waxing as the other manifestations of European empire are waning. Nationalism and something like pan-Islam resurgence are abroad in the world. Most of us in the West know little of the story behind the news. A good deal of it has recently been put into one volume, *Caravan, the Story of the Middle East,* by the anthropologist, Carleton S. Coon.[5] Before we pronounce our theories concerning the contacts of peoples universally true, we would do well to check them against the rich body of pertinent facts in the Middle East.

Maunier [6] and other Frenchmen who have called themselves colonial sociologists have written about the Islamic peoples of Northern Africa and about the half-Muslim tribes further inland. A chief theme of their work has been the conflict btween the demands of French colonial law and those of the sacred Muslim law of the Koran or tribal custom on the peoples of this region. Suppose, for instance, one law says that, on pain of disgrace, you must kill a man who has wronged your clan, while the other law says it will kill you if you carry out this duty. Such dilemmas are among the great themes of the contact of peoples.

Islam and Christianity share Africa as a missionary and racial frontier. The Muslims are said to make little of race or color, so long as people will declare the true faith. Some followers of Allah are more learned and devoted than others. They follow rituals and other duties in fine and pure

---

5. (New York: Henry Holt and Company, 1951.)
6. René Maunier, *Sociologie coloniale.* (Paris: Editions Donat Montchristien, 1932.)

detail, and are at home among sophisticated faithful people in all the cities of Islam. Others are rustic and illiterate peasants or tribesmen who know but little of the Law and who depart in many ways from true practice. These things are important, but race is said not to be. Christianity declares all men equal before God, but Christians established a race-caste line wherever they have gone into Negro Africa. They do it even in the missions—although Christian principles keep breaking through sufficiently to make traders and other European colonials view the missionaries as subversive because so frequently they are advocates of the Negro natives.

The missionary frontier of Christian Europeans and African Negroes has been incidental to modern political and economic conquest of the continent. Here it is that native labor is used on a mammoth scale by European conquering entrepreneurs in extractive industries and in commercial agriculture. Rubber, peanuts, diamonds, gold, and other metals, all are produced by Negro labor organized by Europeans. This is the great place for the student of the detribalization and industrialization of native agricultural, nomadic and forest peoples. For European exploitation has put these people on the move. Sometimes it is their land which is wanted and they must move off. Sometimes, their labor is in demand and various means are used to get it. At any rate, many hundreds of thousands are living away from their native lands and villages. In many cases such people live in compounds segregated from white people. Their movements and activities are limited by law and the police in most regions. There is invariably one law for the white man and another for the black man, occasionally still other laws for colored people (of mixed ancestry) or for non-European immigrants, such as East Indians.

European exploitation has broken up the old tribal units. Generally also the Europeans who control a part of Africa attempt to prevent social and political unity from developing among the natives. There are signs, however, of such new unities bound together by a common sense of oppression, of a common fate now and in the future. Sometimes a people is created by a new common enemy. In the Union of South Africa, at least, events may move quickly thanks to the Nationalist government's race policies. As we write this the Nationalists are advocating that not only the Union but all of Africa be divided into white and non-white territories, and the non-whites be resolutely and systematically removed from the "European areas." Even though this program should never be put fully into effect—as it probably will not—the fact that the diverse non-whites—Negroes of myriad tribes, East Indians, and others—are treated as one, is bound to enter into their conception of themselves and their aspirations.

How many peoples there will be in Africa in the future, no one can say. But it is safe to say that there will be politically active groups with a strong sense of mission to free the dark peoples from domination by the white. What will be their language (since there is no candidate for a national literary language), their territorial limits, their philosophy; who their leaders—these things no one can say.

We are accustomed to think of Asia as the continent of great empires and cities of ancient, grand, but exotic civilizations. The pattern, as J. H. Boeke has shown,[7] rests everywhere upon village agriculture kept at subsistence level by density of population even where yields are high. Urban economy and life have not penetrated far into the country. The peasant folk live in the very shadow of the city. In China and India there are still tribal peoples, not drawn into the main religions and ideologies and not part of the main social structure. In India these tribes are now an object of concern, both because their political allegiance is wanted and because they occupy land, that scarcest of all things in the East. The British in India invented the term "native tribes" to distinguish those peoples not fully Hindu or Muslim, and not part of the caste system. The British policy

---

7. J. H. Boeke, *The Structure of Netherlands Indian Economy* (New York: Institute of Pacific Relations, 1942); also *The Interests of the Voiceless Far East* (Leiden: Universitaire Pers Leiden, 1948).

was to protect them from the caste system and from others who might want their land. It is as if someone were to come to North America to protect the Indians from us. Now that India is free, the matter takes on a new aspect. L. S. Ghurye, a leading Indian anthropologist and sociologist, has written a book, *The Aborigines So-Called and Their Future*,[8] criticizing both the British policy and the British terminology. The term "native tribe" or "aborigines" suggests that these people are more indigenous than other Indians. As for saving them from Hinduism and the caste system, Ghurye maintains that many of them try their best to establish themselves in it, even in a lowly position. For only by getting integrated into the caste system can they hope to share whatever rewards of wealth and social position are to be had by being part of the larger Indian society. Furthermore, Ghurye asks whether the new India can afford to leave such large areas of land to so few people who use it in such a wasteful way. For some of the tribes use the old system of burning over land, cultivating it a little while, and then letting it go fallow again for enrichment, burning, and further cultivation.

It will be interesting to see what will happen in other cases when native sociologists and anthropologists take over the job of describing the people of their own back country, as well as the job of recommending policies concerning them to the eager new governments which are succeeding the colonial administrations. A backward people will not look the same to their sophisticated and reforming countrymen as to the European who sees them both as natives of a colony; the difference of perspective may affect the eyes even of social scientists. It is a change of perspective which will appear larger in the anthropological and sociological work concerning the Far East in the next few years. Until now most anthropology has been written by Europeans visiting in other parts of the world. Some is now being written by Africans about Africans, by Chinese about Chinese. We still await the revolution of comparative social science which may come

---

8. Poona: The Gokhale Institute of Politics and Economics: Publication # 11, 1943.

when Chinese and East Indians start describing the culture of Anglo-Saxon river bottom and houseboat people on the Ohio and Mississippi rivers; or, for that matter, of the farmers of South Dakota and the city dwellers of Chicago.

At any rate, the frontier between larger civilizations and the folk and even tribal cultures is to be found in most of the countries of the Far East. It was reactivated by European empire building which sent entrepreneurs, traders, governmental agents, anthropologists, census takers, and soldiers into remote regions. Rubber and tea plantations brought the usual inter-regional migrations. In many regions the Chinese trader and moneylender stepped into the gap between the European employer and the native labor. Small trading with the native may have been too trifling for the European; or perhaps his standard of living was too high to allow him to live so close to the natives as the Chinese and East Indian small trader does. At any rate, the traders turn up in many regions as a third ethnic group between the European owner-manager of plantations and mines, and the native labor. In this, perhaps, we see a little of the process by which ethnic divisions of labor, and even caste systems, have been built up in the Far East in the past.

Asia is the latest, and perhaps the last, arena of the struggle to establish nation-states. In what was India the conception has become so strongly associated with religion that there are separate Hindu and Muslim states. To make this age-old religious boundary into a thin line on a map people are swarming hither and yon on foot, diplomats are negotiating, commissions investigating, and rival powers carrying on propaganda. It is odd that in this late age the two major attempts to make ethnic and political boundaries coincide— as between Arabs and Jews, and as between Muslim Indians and Hindus—are struggles between religions. They are also in parts of the world where diverse peoples have long lived side by side in the same villages, cities, and regions. What is it that makes it impossible now for these diverse peoples to live in adjacent quarters in the same city and to maintain the old ethnic division of labor? Whatever it is, it is almost certainly due to the stirring up of the East by western economic and political empire building.

The Far East has long been the scene of ethnic mingling. European commercial and political expansion seems to have set the whole mixture seething and heaving again. Population pressures, migrations, technological changes, religious and political movements, all break up the equilibrium. If social scientists are tolerated in such a restless world, and if they have enough sense of mission and thirst for adventure, they will witness in the Far East of the near future some of the most massive dramas of contact in human history. And in the midst of it all, the ancient overland Russian contact with China is being revived with ferocity—and we hear of Chinese laborers being imported into the Silesian industrial country that less than a century ago was exporting labor to western Germany.

Chapter Four

Ecology: Land, Numbers and Survival

By ecology of ethnic or racial contact we mean the processes which determine the relative number, the spatial distribution, and the division of labor between peoples: what they do for and to one another that affects their survival,[1] and their economic behavior.

We talk so much of power nowadays that we are apt to overlook the variety of ways in which people differ from each other and which may influence the nature and course of their relations and even of their survival when in contact with one another. Differences in military disposition, organization, and technology are obviously of great importance. The characteristic modern empire is established when one nation-state extends dominion over territory occupied by other ethnic or racial groups. The territories may be contiguous, as in the case of the old Tsarist Russian empire and the new Soviet empire; or they may be at a distance from

---

1. Pioneering sociological studies of ethnic divisions of labor where capitalism enters colonial regions appear in E. B. Reuter (ed.), *Race and Culture Contacts* (New York: McGraw-Hill Co., 1934), in which papers of the 1933 meeting of the American Sociological Society appear. See especially R. D. McKenzie's paper, "Industrial Expansion and the Interrelations of Peoples," and R. E. Park's, "Race Relations and Certain Frontiers."

the dominant nation-state, as in the British Empire. It is military power which allows a few people thus to rule many.

But the conquest made and contact established, other differences between the peoples affect the course of their relations. Among them are the ways in which they occupy and cultivate land, their ability to recognize and exploit the resources in their environment, and their ways of mobilizing and organizing human effort for these purposes. These differences bring to expression others, as in systems of social organization and sentiments. One people may be bound by rules of caste to avoid certain kinds of work and so find it difficult to compete with men who are free of such taboos. Another people may have strong kin ties which in some circumstances are a handicap. A missionary who introduced improvements in agriculture in a village in India reported that the advantage was lost because relatives swarmed in from the surrounding country to lay claim to their share of the greater yield of grain. But often kinship can give a competitive advantage. A Greek or Chinese peasant has his way paid to America by kinsmen already here; he then works for them for some years, thereby paying the debt, learning the restaurant or laundry business, and earning capital to start his own. It is reported in South Africa that natives converted to the Seventh Day Adventists prosper. The sect is so individualistic that it frees the convert from the web of kinship obligation; only so can he change from the old methods of agriculture to a new, small scale, but more intensive cultivation for the market.

Social structure and sentiments may be regarded as tools, whose value for the survival of the people may be changed by meeting and competing with other peoples who have other forms of social organization and other bodies of sentiment. So regarded, they are factors in the ecology of peoples; that is, in their survival in relation to their physical and human environments. For people of one culture or race become a crucial and fateful part of the environment to which other peoples must adjust if they are to survive. When contacts become such that one people must adjust itself to another, every feature of the culture and social organization of both may have a part in the outcome.

A relatively few men with the capital and knowledge of one economic system behind them may reorganize the economic and social life of great numbers of people of another economy and technology. A handful of missionaries may profoundly affect the social organization, the ways of working, and the wants of a whole people. Traders may likewise make some of their arts obsolete by introducing new articles; to buy the new articles the local people must make changes in their economy. Or perhaps the traders buy from them something which they previously produced only in that small quantity required for their own consumption. Invaders may find a native population simply a nuisance since they occupy land which the newcomers want to cultivate or from which they want to extract some resource. Or it may be, as in the early times of the Spanish conquest in America, that the natives have portable wealth which the invaders want to take away. Even in such cases the invaders may eventually see the native populations themselves as a resource or a market, and new relations may grow out of exploiting them as such. Thus, in South Africa the Boers wanted the land of the Natives and took it. They used some Natives as farm labor; eventually, mining and other industries created the need for a large labor supply and measures were taken to loosen them from their villages for the purpose.

The distribution of the races over the earth has sometimes been accounted for by saying that some of them are better adapted to certain climates than are others. It used to be said in this country that Negroes died of tuberculosis when they came North. Carleton Coon believes blondes don't survive in the sunnier parts of the Middle East. White men—it has been said—cannot live, work, and multiply under the tropical sun, while people of more pigmented skins can. Grenfell White has reviewed the theories and the facts in his *The White Man in the Tropics.*

In fact, the white man does go into the tropics, with mos-

quito net, sun helmet, snakeproof boots and a quinine jag.
The dangers of the big game hunt, of the expedition (bo-
tanical, prospecting, anthropological, or punitive) he will
and does face. In them he plays a role to his taste. But he
doesn't like to meet the sun bare-skinned or the jungle barehanded, as do many natives of the tropics. We do not know
whether white men in any number would survive in the
Amazon Valley with the culture of the wandering native
tribes of the region; or whether people of European race
would work, survive, and multiply in the villages of India
with the there prevailing culture and technology. To find
out, some considerable number of Europeans would have to
change their attitudes toward life.

The Western European peoples and peoples of that extraction in North America and elsewhere have achieved low
death rates; their birth rates have become correspondingly
low, so that if in these countries there is a given excess of
births over deaths, it is an excess of one small quantity over
a still smaller one. In other parts of the world both birth and
death rates are much higher. It is as if the European attitude
toward life was stingy and saving—except for a vast tolerance
of death when dealt by war or automobiles or airplanes. We
hesitate to let children be born, and we protect them carefully from disease. Other peoples are more prodigal of life.
Perhaps it is the attitude as much as a pale skin which keeps
masses of white men out of the tropics. And here we are
speaking of differences of standards of living, or, let us say,
standard of life, as they affect the biological processes which
determine the number and distribution of people.

When races meet in the same territory, or become part
of the same survival system, we may reasonably expect that
the balance of births and deaths of each will be affected.[2]
An invaded people may be reduced by killing, by new dis-
eases, by disorders brought on by change of diet, by loss of
land, game, or morale. Sometimes settlers breed and mul-

---

2. Bernhard Lothar Hörmann, *Extinction and Survival: A Study of the
Reaction of Aboriginal Populations to European Expansion* (Ph.D. dissertation, Department of Sociology, University of Chicago, 1949).

tiply mightily in a new country, where they have plenty of space and food, as did our ancestors here and the Boers in South Africa. Perhaps there is a cycle of influence of European populations on colonial ones. The first effect of the European invasion and settlement on the natives is often decimation. The settlers, however, being more prosperous and in a more open society than at home, multiply. But the invading population reaches the limit of easily-obtainable resources, loses the pioneering spirit, and goes back to the careful, conservative system of small families. Meanwhile the native population gets some increase of the means of life and enough improvement of medicine from their contact with the Europeans to reduce their death rate significantly. With the death-rate dam lower, the flood of births rapidly increases the population. In the meantime, some natives enter more fully into the new economy of the invaders, adopt their standards of living, and so begin both to demand higher wages and to reduce the size of their families. Thus there may slowly set in a reduction of the rate of increase of the native population. But there is a period when the rate of increase of the invading population has become low while that of the native population is still high. Death rates seem to go down sooner than birth rates. In this phase the relative numbers of the two kinds of people can change drastically. Whether many cases actually show these changes in the order given, or not, this presentation suggests the ways in which the biological balance of one people interacts with that of another. There are several cases which do appear to have run through such a cycle; among them, apparently, is Algiers.[3]

One may think of the whole world as a biological community in which a series of such cycles are run through, with resulting massive changes in the relative numbers of the various races. The expansion of the people of Europe over the earth allowed them to increase greatly in number. They

3. Cf. G. Mesnard, "La régression relative des Européens en Algérie," *Congrès International de la Population, 1937*, VI. *Démographie de la France d'Outremer* (Paris: Hermann *et* Cie.; 1938), pp. 11-14.

then reduced their rate of increase, but as a result of their activities the populations of Asia and Africa have had a great spurt of growth.

These are processes of competition, not in the sense of traders competing through smart bargaining in a market, but in the sense of the biological struggle for life. Some people occupy land closely and spread out, like grass, from the root, and at the expense of others. Some prefer certain kinds of soils, and manage to find and stick to them. It has been said of Germans in this country that they settle only in limestone country, and that generally they waited until the more adventurous Yankees had opened up the country and tried out the soil. Once established, however, the Germans stuck to the land and kept to something like European standards of rotation of crops and fertilizing. It is said in many parts of the northern states that a German farmer builds a fine barn while the old-stock Yankee farmer first built a fine house. This saying is used to account for the Germans managing to survive on the land and to buy out other farmers.

Certain rural sectarian farmers demonstrate clearly the process by which one group may spread and displace others. Their religion makes them live plainly; they may—in some sects—not own a car nor have electric lights in their houses, go to theaters or wear bright clothing. While this no doubt saves them money, it also keeps them immune to the ways of the world. They discourage their children from going to school long enough to be much exposed to outsiders. The boys stay at home and help with the chores and so learn to farm. They participate in an intensive system of family and neighborhood mutual aid. At only one point are such communities progressive—in their methods of agriculture and of selling their produce. By a combination of excellent farming, low expenditures, and effective mutual aid they can buy up land for a son who comes of age. He has already contributed to the prosperity of the family by his labor. Even if he were a little inclined to waiver in his adherence to the peculiar faith, the reward of a good farm might hold him.

A member of the Dunker sect says the following story is current in a community of that sect in Pennsylvania: A farmer and his wife went to the bank with a barrel of money to pay for a farm for one of their sons. When they got the proper sum counted out there was still a good deal left in the bottom of the barrel. The farmer exclaimed to his wife, "Mamma, we must have brought the wrong barrel!" One may say that these people compete with their religion, with their very other-worldliness—a very earthy other-worldliness, to be sure.

In eastern Canada and down into New England French Canadians spread in similar fashion at the expense of English-speaking Protestant farmers. In this case the English are probably right in saying that the French won't get as much off the land as they did, that the wood will be cut off, and that the buildings will run down. Yet the French have displaced the English steadily for more than a century. Perhaps the English farmer is too ambitious for his children, and finds himself without a successor. He has only a son or two, anyway. The French-Canadian farmer's son—he was one of several and so had to leave home—comes to work for the English farmer. He stays on and it may be buys the farm when the English owner dies and the heirs want to divide the estate. He rears a large family, who work at home and so make it possible to run it without too much capital. Then, in the French-Canadian way, he gives the land to one son only to avoid losing it altogether—for he knows of old that a family farm won't support two families.

It is likely that one of the significant elements in the competition of people for land is their way of meeting the crises of the turn of generations.[4] If a farm is of just the size to support a family, it can scarcely support all the sons with

---

4. Horace Miner, *St. Denis; a French-Canadian Rural Parish* (Chicago: University of Chicago Press, 1939; Conrad Arensberg and Solon T. Kimball, *Family and Community in Ireland* (Cambridge: Harvard University Press, 1940); Leonard J. Salter, Jr., *Land Tenure in Process: A Study of Farm Ownership and Tenancy in a Lafayette County (Wis.) Township* (Madison: Agricultural Experiment Station of the University of Wisconsin, Research Bulletin No. 146, February 1943; also Kenneth H. Parsons and Eliot O. Waples,

their families. Yet the farmer may have several sons, all of whom he loves and all of whom would like to have the farm. Certain societies have said the eldest son shall have the family land and the house and tools necessary to working it. The Chinese, on the other hand, divide it, with the result that in a couple of generations the holdings are so small that most people lose what little they have to someone who manages to buy it up and start the cycle over again.[5] In this country the sentiment for equal division is strong. One son may keep the farm but give a mortgage to his fellow-heirs for their share; the owner may thus be so indebted that he loses all if there is the least strain. We tend to bring the whole estate to a cash expression at every turn of the generations. The French Canadians, many European peasants and the German and Swiss farmers in Wisconsin avoid this by a bond or contract by which the father, when ready to retire, gives the land to one son who agrees to provide for the old people and to do certain things for the other children. The others, however, must leave. How many others there are and what happens to them may have significant effects on the spatial distribution of ethnic groups and on their competition in industry.

The excess sons of French-Canadian families and their descendants form a large part of the labor supply of New England, and are still pouring into the rapidly growing industries of Canada. Indeed their case is a classic illustration of how peoples compete with their sentiments, customs and institutions as well as with their technical skills and money; for it was precisely the growing demand for labor as New England and later the Province of Quebec itself became industrialized, that kept the traditional form of rural inheritance viable in Quebec. Though the birth rate has long been one of the highest in the Western World, the number of Quebec farms remains virtually unchanged and the rural

Keeping the Farm in the Family: A Study of Ownership Processes in a Low Tenancy Area of Eastern Wisconsin, Research Bulletin No. 157, September 1945.

5. Hsiao-Tung Fei and Chih-I Chang, *Earthbound China.* (Chicago: University of Chicago Press, 1945.)

population is static. (In 1931, for example, the rural and village population numbered just 238 more than it had been in 1871!) This was only possible because the excess children have been able to find a livelihood in factory work.[6] But—and this is what makes it interesting to us—this industry which had the effect of conserving the family system, was itself established by ethnic strangers. In the mill towns the ex-*habitants* found bosses and fellow-workers who were Yankees, or Englishmen, or—equally alien—Canadians from Ontario. Eventually, in consequence of the rural land system, the uprooted French Canadian became a proletarian, spoke English after a fashion, went to movies made in Hollywood, and exchanged the delights of home-grown tobacco for advertised brands. The mill towns of New England and Quebec became the frontier between the Anglo-Saxon, Protestant, city man of modern industry and the country-bred carrier of the Catholic faith, the French language, the rustic arts and the ancient ways.

The rural ethnic boundaries of North America have always been in flux and still are. In some regions the first settlers neglected some types of soil or terrain, which were later taken over by other ethnic groups. Thus Yankees coming west settled the higher parts of lower Michigan and northern Illinois, leaving the black muck of the swamps for Dutch immigrants who came a generation later. The Dutch know about gardening in the wet soil. On the west coast, land-hungry Japanese gardeners (for Japanese farming is essentially gardening) got out of working for others as fast as they could. They did it by growing berries and small fruits on land that the Caucasian settlers did not bother with. Both the Dutch and the Japanese then worked up and out toward other land and other occupations, as enterprising people generally do.

In other cases one ethnic group wears out the land by a mode of cultivation, only to be followed by a second ethnic

---

6. See Everett C. Hughes, "Industry and the Rural System in Quebec," *Canadian Journal of Economics and Political Science*, IV, No. 3 (August, 1938), 341-49.

group which can survive because of a lower standard of living or different mode of cultivation. Or it may be a change in markets. The Yankee farmer did not generally make the change from field farming to market gardening required by the growth of cities in New England. He took his profits and went to the city, or stayed in the country and went to pot. He left it to Portuguese, Poles, and Italians to break their backs—and their wives' backs—and make small fortunes by growing vegetables. A similar succession has occurred around most large northern cities in America.

Technological changes and changes in mode of cultivation may be accompanied by changes in racial or ethnic balance of the population. Thus in parts of the South cotton lands are being turned into grazing or dairy lands. Whatever may be the case in the future, cotton has in the past required many hands of all ages for hoeing and picking. Dairying does not. Mr. Samuel Adams reports that the white Alabama landowner who previously did not want Negroes to get too much schooling, for fear of spoiling them as cotton-hands, is now looking for that one well-educated, reliable Negro couple he needs to look after his dairy herd, and is more than willing to give them a good house to live in and to encourage the kind of school that will keep them content to remain.

On ethnic rural frontiers of contact all over the earth, the deadly serious drama of competition and succession is forever being played. Sometimes peasants' revolts and other forms of agrarian unrest compel attention to the human cost of the meeting and melting of peoples; but more characteristically it is a silent struggle. We shall pass now to a frontier of contact where peoples are, on the whole, more clamorous and more conscious of their own roles and their own fate. This is the frontier of industry.

Chapter Five

Industrial Revolutions and Ethnic Frontiers

In modern times representatives of the western world have gone out to other parts of the globe armed with powerful technology, correspondingly powerful forms of organization for work and exchange, and with the determination to draw resources, land, and people into their great world economy. If political and social revolutions were necessary to bring about industrial revolutions, they have not hesitated to make them. Often, indeed, they have been only half aware of the catastrophic effect of what they regarded as merely "doing business." Thus the major cultural contacts of modern times have brought an industrial revolution, a revolution in ways of working and in the institutions relating to work, to one or more of the peoples involved. Conversely, industrial revolutions create ethnic and racial frontiers, for in no major industrial region of the world has one ethnic group furnished the whole labor force, from managers down to unskilled labor—a circumstance about which we shall have more to say later.

The mother-countries of modern expanding industry were those of western Europe and the United States. The active carriers, the people who made the industrial revolutions, were of these countries, and were mainly Protestant Christians, with some Catholics and Jews. All worked with and further developed the basic complex of institutions known as capitalism. Japan eventually became a center from which industrial revolutions were made, using the same institutional complex with some modifications. The last active center of industrial expansion is Soviet Russia, whose impulse seems greatest just when that of the older centers is on the wane. Perhaps it is more accurate to say that some of the former industrial colonies have matured, and no longer welcome either control or personnel from the old centers. In fact, the people of a country that has been an industrial colony sometimes, like impatient adolescents, revolt against the control from the founding center before they accumulate the skill and capital goods to carry on alone. It has been one of the apparent anomalies of the rise of modern industry that it should so often have involved ethnic conflict, for industry of this kind depends upon and pretends to a high degree of the application of reason, while matters of race and nation are essentially sentimental. The labor movement, which has repeatedly affirmed the common interests and brotherhood of all workers, has again and again been caught on the hook of race, ethnic kind, and even of religion.

Some of the most significant questions, both about race relations and about the relations of industry and society in general, are raised in discussions combining the two: race relations in industry. This is a subject being currently explored by American sociologists with the object of learning how to make fuller use of our labor force, regardless of race or ethnic distinction. In the remarks which follow these two themes are played in counterpoint.[1] For whenever one scratches a problem of racial and ethnic relations he uncovers problems concerning society itself: and in this case concerning industry and society.

---

1. This chapter contains substantially Everett C. Hughes' paper "Queries Concerning Industry and Society Growing out of Study of Ethnic Relations in Industry," read at the annual meeting of the American Sociological So-

Three sweeping statements may be made which are germane to the whole problem of ethnic relations in industrial economies.

The first is that industry is always and everywhere a grand mixer of peoples. War and trade mix them too, but chiefly as precursors to the deeper revolutions of work and production in which the more fateful mixing occurs. In no considerable industrial region of the world, to repeat, has an indigenous population supplied the whole working force. Some of it comes from such a distance as to be noticeably different from the local people. The resulting ethnic differences within the industrial population may be small, as between people from the various parts of Great Britain, or as between Yankees and Southerners in this country; or great, as between Poles, eastern Germans, and western Germans in the Ruhr and Rheinland, or as between English and French Canadians in Quebec. They may be extreme, as between South African natives and Europeans, or between North Americans and native Indians of Peru. In short, the differences may range in magnitude from those between regions of the same country, through those between different European nationalities, to those between European and non-European, the latter being most extreme when some of the people are of tribal cultures whose institutions of property and work are entirely different from those known in Europe.

Industrial regions vary also as to the positions of local people relative to those of immigrants. At one pole are those regions in which the working force is built around a nucleus of native controlling and technical personnel and skilled workers, and where successive waves of immigrants enter the working force at the bottom of the skill hierarchy. At the other extreme are those regions in which the controlling and highly skilled nucleus goes out to establish industry in a remote, unindustrialized part of the world; the labor is recruited either from a native population, or—and this is com-

---

ciety held in Chicago, December, 1948, and published in the *American Sociological Review*, XIV, No. 2 (April, 1949), pp. 211-20.

mon—is imported from still other ethnic areas. It thus may happen that practically the whole industrial personnel is alien to the region, while the various ranks are alien to each other, as in the mines and plantations of the Malay peninsula.

Finally, the industrial regions vary as to the kinds of industrial and social structures which develop and in the degrees of upward mobility possible for various racial and ethnic elements of the working force. Again, at one pole are the somewhat open structures in which there is a theoretical, although practically limited, possibility for a person of any ethnic kind to fill any position; at the other, rigid systems of stratification in which the people of each ethnic group are limited to a narrow range of jobs or ranks. Each of these kinds of variation has its accompaniments in the industrial community, and eventually in the political and social conflicts, alignments, and movements which follow the development of industry.

The second sweeping statement is that modern industry, by virtue of being the great mixer, has inevitably been a colossal agent of racial, ethnic, and religious segregation. For segregation, if it means something more than that isolation in which the peculiarities of race and culture develop, refers to some degree of functional separation of different kinds of people within a common system. Industry brings people together and sorts them out for various kinds of work; the sorting will, where the mixture is new, of necessity follow racial and ethnic lines. For cultures (and when races first meet they are always unlike in culture) differ in nothing more than in the skills, work habits, and goals which they instil into the individual. These differences may tend to disappear in the course of industrial experience, although segregation may tend to keep them alive in some modified form for a long time. At any rate, there is not yet —even among the older industrial regions, where ethnic differences have been reduced by common experience and intermarriage—one in which one may not discern some deviation from chance expectation in the distribution of ethnic and religious groups among the various kinds of work and the several ranks of industrial organizations.[2] In Montreal, for example, 74% of the semi-skilled and 69% of the skilled workers in manufacturing, but only 34% of the sales force and 22% of people in managerial positions were French, a few years ago. The English Canadians, who are later arrivals in Quebec, were over-represented at the top and underrepresented at the bottom.[3]

The third of the sweeping statements is that industry is almost universally an agent of racial and ethnic discrimination. There is no question about it if we take the word *discrimination* in its basic sense of the action of making distinctions. For those who hire industrial help must nearly always choose from among people who are not all alike ethnically, and very often from among ethnic groups whose industrial experience and training are far from equal. Furthermore, when industry actively seeks labor from new sources, it generally has to make an ethnic choice.

In sociological language, discrimination has taken another meaning: that those who pick people for jobs consider, intentionally or unwittingly, traits not directly relevant to work. If we accept this meaning, industry is still almost universally an agent of ethnic discrimination. In all industrial regions, again including the oldest, there is current among managers, foremen, and industrial workers, a body of opinion and lore concerning the work capacities and habits of various ethnic groups. Insofar as such belief and lore do not correspond to verifiable fact, they point to discrimina-

2. This is so obviously true in North America as to need no proof. For evidence concerning western Germany see: Wilhelm Brepohl, *Der Aufbau des Ruhrvolkes in Zuge der Ost-West-Wanderung* (Recklinghausen: Bitter & Co., 1948); Everett C. Hughes, "The Industrial Revolution and the Catholic Movement in Germany," *Social Forces*, XIV (Dec., 1935). There are marked differences between the positions of Flemings and Walloons in Belgium; Protestant and Catholic in Holland; Flemings, Italians, etc., and French in France. It is commonly said that such differences of distribution still exist as between Welsh, Scottish, Irish, and English of various regions of the British Isles.

3. Cf. Everett C. Hughes and Margaret L. McDonald, "French and English in the Economic Structure of Montreal," *Canadian Journal of Economics and Political Science*, VII, No. 4 (November, 1941), 493-505.

tion. Certainly they hinder clear perception of the differences between individuals of a given ethnic or racial group. In some industrial regions, discrimination is openly defended; in a few, enforced by law.

We have defined industrial segregation as deviation from chance in the distribution of people of various ethnic groups among the positions in industry. Discrimination we have defined as consideration of racial, ethnic, or religious traits in selection of workers even when the traits are not known to be relevant to work behavior. But segregation is not of itself evidence of discrimination. For there are undoubtedly cases in which even the most objective and sharp selection of workers by known or probable work performance would result in racial and ethnic segregation. On the other hand, we do not know how long it would take, under an aggressively objective policy, for all racial and ethnic disparities in job distribution to disappear. The truth is that no one has worked out a statistical device for establishing the existence or degree of ethnic discrimination. It would be very difficult to do so. For a given organization may have a great variety of jobs and positions, each of which has its own complex of activities and skills, and consequently of required training and experience. The positions have each their own rate of turnover, so that they vary in their sensitivity to ethnic change in the labor supply. Past discrimination leaves its mark in varying degree and for varying lengths of time. But the lack of such an index need not worry students of the problem unduly. For discrimination is generally admitted, although it may be called by other names when discrimination becomes a bad word. In fact, the evidence of recent studies indicates that at least an unconscious discrimination tends to permeate industrial organizations even in the rare moments when conscious effort is made to avoid it.

It is an interesting and apparently paradoxical observation that modern capitalistic industry, which has developed a strong, sometimes ruthless ideology of indifference to persons, of choice of the best article for the purpose, and of the best man for the job, and which has shown a great drive, almost a mission, to sweep away beliefs, customs and institutions which stand in the way of industrial development, should also have become not merely—as one might have expected—an aggressive and grandiose mixer of peoples, but also a great and sometimes stubborn agent of racial and ethnic discrimination and a breeder of racial doctrines and stereotypes. The American industrial executive—and he is probably like such personages wherever they are to be found —prides himself on his progressive experimental attitude toward industrial processes; and, at the same time, on his ability to recognize a promising worker when he sees one. But Hermann Feldman surveyed racial realities in American industry and found that nearly all employers had firm convictions about the industrial aptitudes of men of various nationalities and races, but no real evidence. "Actual analysis of the comparative capacity of different racial groups is," he remarked, "not a part of the practice of industrial concerns."[4] This raises the general question whether, and under what circumstances, modern industry is really guided by the impersonal concepts of the market and efficiency in choosing and assigning its labor force.

Another tenet of the ideology of modern industrial management has been that all barriers to free movement of labor should be removed in the interest of its economic use. This appeared in the movement to remove restrictions against internal migration in the early days of the industrial revolution in Europe, and in the insistence on treating each worker as an individual whose employment could be terminated at will by either party without interference of any third party. With reference to this tenet we may ask: To what extent and under what circumstances *does* industry rely on purely economic means and incentives applied to freely moving individuals to get and keep a labor supply, and under what circumstances does it use or encourage essentially political means, such as restriction of movement, fixed terms of employment, or differential rules governing the movement and

---

4. *Racial Factors in American Industry* (New York: Harper and Bros., 1931), p. 192.

activities of certain categories of people? There are other
questions like these concerning the behavior of industrial
management in various social settings. We believe it one of
the major tasks of people interested in a sociological view of
industry to seek the answers to these questions, and that the
way to do it is to compare the ways of industry in a variety of
settings, including a variety of inter-racial and inter-ethnic
settings.

A first and evident comparison is that between the mother-
countries of modern technology and industrial institutions,
including their closer satellites, and the outlying, newer industrial regions which we' may call colonial whether they
are so in a political sense or not.

In the mother-countries (England, Belgium, Holland,
Germany, parts of other western European countries, and
North America), those who manage industry and perform its
higher technical functions are native, as are also the central
core of skilled workers. At least, they are native to this general area and feel themselves at home in it. Even within
these areas, however, managers and technicians may be ethnically somewhat strange to the particular smaller regions in
which they work. Many of the founders, engineers, and
skilled workers of the early industries in the German Ruhr
came from Britain and Belgium where coal mining and the
iron industry had first developed machinery. It was not long,
however, before Germany could supply such people in numbers sufficient for her own industry and for export.

There has been a constant flow of managers, accountants,
engineers and skilled workers from these mother countries
to the outlying newly industrialized regions of the Western
world itself, as well as to the colonial regions. This movement takes them, and the industries they operate, into
regions where they are ethnically strange enough for it to be
remarked by themselves and by the native population. Examples are the central and eastern countries of Europe, the
French parts of Canada, and even our Southern states. As the
prime movers of industry get out into the less industrially-
minded parts of the Western world one begins to hear from

them those impatient complaints about the perversity of local institutions and people which they utter more openly in colonial regions.

In the older industrial regions of the mother-countries the rank and file working force was generally built about a nucleus of people native to the region and of the same ethnic kind as management. But as industry grew, large and long-continued internal migration and immigration from other countries were necessary to keep up and expand the working force. The consequent ethnic differences are of the order of national differences within the European world. Of the mother-countries, only the United States has recruited a sizable part of its labor from outside the European cultures and races. Such people, Negroes, Orientals, and Latin American mestizos, were generally brought here as labor, not for manufacturing but for industrial agriculture and construction work, just as in the colonial areas. It has been only after a long experience in the Euro-American culture and economy, and usually after turnover of generations, that people of other than European ancestry have found their way into the labor force of American manufacturing industry.

When industry is brought to a previously unindustrialized region or community of the Western world, it may find there already established middle classes, or even an aristocracy, based on land, commerce and the professions. The leaders of these classes may be jealous of the power and incomes of the newcomers who control industry. The jealousy is perhaps more apparent, although not necessarily more acute, when the new industrial leaders are ethnically different from the local people of influence. The latter, however, often encourage the coming of industry in the hope that it will enhance the value of their land and enlarge their businesses and their professional clienteles. Some combination of cooperation and antagonism between the middle class and the new industrial leaders develops. This becomes a major theme of local politics. Young men on their way to success in the older system of things may feel especially threatened and fight the

newcomers in the name of the local culture or ethnic group:
others may seek their fortunes in the new order.

To this is added the politics of labor, as the industrial
working force takes form and becomes defined in its own
eyes and those of management and the local non-industrial
middle class. Some of the workers, whether native or immigrant, will try to rise in the industrial structure; their success or failure will almost certainly become symbolically important to the workers at large. If it be failure, the flames
of ethnic consciousness will be fanned thereby, and local
politics will reflect the fire. There may develop a labor movement which defines its enemy, management, in racial or
ethnic terms, and which may, at the same time, endeavor to
keep out workers of other ethnic or racial kinds. Since these
are areas in which all, or nearly all, classes of people are accustomed to take some part in politics, and therefore may be
quickly mobilized against industry, management cannot ignore local politics. The various political alignments which
develop in such industrial communities, and the circumstances which change them have been talked of, and have,
in a few cases, been described and analyzed.[5] There is need
of systematic comparison of them in a variety of situations.

Although it must reckon with unfavorable alignments and
opposition, industry can count on finding in the Western
world the basic matrix of law, institutions, and ideologies
in which the special institutions of capitalistic industry grew
up. It is a fair generalization that in the mother-countries
industry prefers as little interference of government as possible, excepting only use of the police power to protect their
"property" and "right to operate," and of legislation to protect markets. In such countries industry is, as a rule, against
attempts to restrict the flow of labor into and out of the region. An exception appears in marginal areas which share
some of the characteristics of the colonial world; such as in
the southern United States, where an industrial agriculture
had developed slavery and when that was abolished, other

---

5. E.g., W. L. Warner and J. O. Low, *The Social System of a Modern
Factory* (New Haven: Yale University Press, 1947).

devices for holding people to their jobs—a pattern taken over to some extent by early manufacturing industries in the region.

At the opposite pole from the Western mother-countries of modern industry stand the colonial areas of the world whither men of European extraction have gone or sent their agents to gather and fetch to world markets vegetable and mineral products wanted for consumption or manufacture in the industrial mother-countries.[6] The first capitalistic industrial enterprises in such regions are usually plantations or mines, which marshal large numbers of native people to labor under what is to them an alien system.

Often not enough native people can be immediately recruited to meet the newcomers' demand; in this case, laborers may be imported under indenture or contract from some other non-industrial, non-European country; generally, the imported labor has come from among the non-tribal peoples of Asia where large masses of landless people accustomed to wage-work are willing to hire themselves out for a period of years without hope of advancement. When their terms of work are up they often go into small trading or commercial farming. They thus become a middle caste of small entrepreneurs, as have the Chinese in the East Indies and the East Indians in South Africa.

The natives themselves are often not accustomed to individual wage work, at least as a continued and sole means of getting a living. They may have worked only as members of communities, their tasks and their rewards determined by their places in a social system. Hence they are not always willing to work for long periods, if at all, in the new enterprises. In such case the political force of the colonial power is used to recruit and hold workers. Among people who live by the labor of their own hands, plus a few articles got by

---

6. For a general definition of colonial status see Raymond Kennedy, "The Colonial Crisis and the Future," in R. Linton, *The Science of Man in the World Crisis* (New York, 1945). He notes that Japan is (or was) the one non-European nation to have developed modern political and economic colonies, and that these colonies showed the essential features of colonies of European countries.

barter, money is no temptation to labor. And one device to make them wish for money—widely used in South Africa— has been the head tax enforced by the colonial government. It was effective because it could not be paid in chickens or salt but had to be paid in the currency of the new system, which was procurable only by work for wages. The erstwhile tribesman had to leave his family and his village and spend at least as much time in wage work as it took to raise the tax. For that time, he lived near the mine or plantation which so aggressively invited his employment. And this naturally led to another invention—the labor compound—where native workers not only had to live but which in some instances they were not at liberty to leave. Penal sanctions could be applied to those who left work without authorization.

Restrictions on movement in and out of the district and, earlier, colonial chattel slavery served the same end.[7] In short, the usual economic incentives do not always bring in a labor supply. Industry departs from its mother-country practice of encouraging free movement of labor, and uses the police power instead. The problem of early industry in England was to make the people free to move from parish to parish so that they might be available to industry; one could assume that the poor would use the freedom in a way profitable to industry. In colonial regions, that assumption proves not true, and there is a complete reversal of tactic.

This raises the whole question of the relation of industry to the law, institutions, and mores of the communities and regions where it establishes enterprises. In the Western world the representatives of industry claim to believe in as little government as possible, and generally claim to respect the mores, religion, and social beliefs of the communities in

7. For material on this subject see: J. H. Boeke, *The Structure of the Netherlands Indian Economy* (New York: Institute of Pacific Relations, 1942); John A. Noon, *Labor Problems of Africa* (Philadelphia: University of Pennsylvania Press, 1944); Sheila van der Horst, *Native Labour in South Africa* (London: Oxford University Press, 1942); Sydney Olivier, *White Capital and Coloured Labour* (London, 1906), and *The Anatomy of African Misery* (London, 1927); James Bryce, *The Relations Between the Advanced and the Backward Races of Mankind* (London, 1902).

which they operate. Indeed, local custom and belief are often plead by industrial management as their reason for racial and ethnic discrimination and segregation. On the other hand, industry has eaten away at many customs and beliefs by its very insistence on continuous operation. But in the main the law, sentiments, and symbols of the community are essentially those of the leaders of industry themselves. In the purely colonial regions they are not. Local institutions and law may not allow for the kind of organization that industry regards essential to its operation; and the policing power may be neither strong enough nor properly minded to support industry. The evidence from colonial situations makes it appear that where the local legal and institutional framework stands in the way, industry is prepared to modify it as much as need be. This it does by support of imperial interference with local authority. An additional means is the establishment of separate industrial communities in which industry and its representatives exercise political and police functions over their employees: thus the familiar colonial institutions of the labor compound, the plantation, and that institution of areas marginal to the colonial world, the company town. The plantation, the compound, and the kind of company town one finds on the remote frontiers of the industrial world are all departures in practice from the doctrine that industry controls only the working time and activity of the worker. The whole life of the worker is kept under surveillance, and the right of entry to and departure from the community is controlled by the employer in measure that varies from slight to complete and absolute. Sydney Olivier, a British colonial official who speculated on what he saw in the West Indies and Jamaica, asked himself why the worker in Europe could be counted on to turn up at the employment gate without force while in Africa the employer thinks it necessary to resort to legal and police measures to keep a labor force. He might also have asked under what circumstances the employer will resort to other than the economic means of offering wages to get his labor force, and when he thinks himself justified in controlling their lives outside work.

One of our tasks should be the close analysis of the behavior of industrial management toward local law, institutions, and beliefs in a whole series of situations, from those in which local society is apparently most favorable to industry to those in which it is least favorable. At the colonial pole we get evidence of a belief in the divine right of industry to modify any society as much as need be to allow it to exploit local markets, resources and labor; perhaps it is undertaken with the least pang when the local people and culture are of some kind with whom industrial managers feel little human identification. This is one meaning of the "white man's burden."

On the other hand, it may turn out that industry will lose its sense of identification with the law, institutions and people of an older industrial community if they develop in a way unfavorable to industry beyond some point of tolerance. It is possible that law, institutions, and sentiments are most favorable to industry in Western communities with well-developed concepts of the law relating to property, organization of voluntary corporations, free individual contract, and the like, but not yet highly nor long industrialized—communities still virgin, but ripe for willing embrace.

To resume our comparison: as a result of the importation of labor from other regions, the industrial hierarchy in colonial areas often consists of several ethnic groups, each of which performs some rather distinct function.[8] The new recruits of each group come into the structure at a given level and tend to remain there. There is no ladder of promotion by small rungs from the bottom to the top of the structure. Mobility tends to occur mainly by leaving the industrial organization for some new commercial or service function brought into being by the social revolution accompanying

---

8. R. D. McKenzie, "Cultural and Racial Difference as Bases of Human Symbiosis," in K. Young (ed.), *Social Attitudes* (New York, 1931); Sydney Olivier, *op. cit.*, Sheila van der Horst, *op. cit.*

the growth of the new economic system. There is almost complete absence of the kind of industrial mobility which is so strong in the ideology of industry in the Western countries.

A related feature of the colonial regions, well described by J. H. Boeke [9] in his works on the Dutch East Indies, is that the native labor is for a long time only half way in the new system. When not working in it for wages they are absorbed again and kept by the familial, tribal, or village societies to which they still belong. In course of time the power of the native society and economy to re-absorb the industrial workers declines, through loss of land to the new system of things, or through pressure of population. At the same time some of the natives become so weaned from their mother culture as to have no wish to return to it. Their goals are already turned toward the new life. Thus there grows up a group of people who are completely dependent upon the new industrial system, people who—when not working for wages—must now be considered the unemployed of the new system. Such people are inclined to become discontent, to demand a new and higher scale of wages so that they can buy the consumers' goods of the new system, and even to demand that they be allowed to climb higher in the industrial hierarchy.

Andrew W. Lind has given a classic description of this cycle: "The process by which Hawaii imports large numbers of unskilled laborers from various sections of the globe, exploits their labor power for a few years on the sugar and pineapple plantations, and at the same time initiates them into the great American scramble for a place at the top of the economic ladder, is apparently irreversible and is cumulative in its exactions upon the existing economy and culture. Each new generation of plantation workers occasions an addition to the surplus of competitors for the preferred positions within the system, not alone by the graduation of the majority of its number to the ranks of non-plantation pursuits, but even more by the creation of a second genera-

9. J. H. Boeke, *op. cit.*

tion even more thoroughly innoculated with the American success virus." [10]

A similar cycle occurs even in the mother-countries of industry when people of "backward" rural regional or ethnic elements are drawn into the less skilled jobs of industry in times of acute labor shortage. We have seen it in the United States in the case of the rural Southern people, both Negro and white; and in Canada, in the case of "backwoods" people from Quebec and the Maritime provinces. It is a process which contains the problem of hidden social subsidies to industry, and the question whether industry can maintain the level of profit which it has come to expect when all such hidden subsidy has wasted away and the population must be kept alive on industrial income even when not working for industry.

In the colonial regions there is either no middle class of natives in the European sense (South Africa), or the middle class (as in India or China) is far removed from any place in industry or control over it. The middle classes may pick up some crumbs of prosperity or power from the presence of the new economic order, or they may be threatened and destroyed by it. In either case they may be without political power. The masses are at first politically inactive, but may begin to show signs of forming new groups, of a feeling of nationality where once there had been only tribal or village solidarity. A new nationalism may arise, and economic and ethnic unrest may be joined in it—whence that confusion of racial and class conflict so common in the colonial areas of the world.

Within industry itself one finds in these colonial areas almost no admission of the native population to the inner and higher positions of prestige and control. The tendency to exclude ethnically alien elements is here seen in its extreme; or perhaps it is only more visible because of race and the sharp cultural distinctions between the working many and

---

10. *Economic and Racial Invasion in Hawaii* (University of Chicago Libraries, 1936), p. 404. See also his *An Island Community: Ecological Succession in Hawaii* (Chicago: University of Chicago Press, 1938).

the managing few. Where this line of effective exclusion is drawn depends upon circumstances and upon the nature of the industry. In South African mining, white men came from England to do the skilled work at first; now that a native labor force which could do the work has been developed, the politically active white men use the full power of the state and of racial solidarity to preserve their own monopoly. The line is held at the gate to skilled work; industry puts up with it at great cost. In other cases the line is drawn at supervision and authority. In others the main concern is to keep merely the higher control of policy and money in the hands of representatives of the dominant European group.

Here we meet that peculiar phenomenon, the straw-boss, and can see his essential function. A native is given supervision over native workers; or a person of some ethnic group alien both to management and the mass of workers is given this function. The notion is that such a person will know the peculiar ways of the workers, and will deal with them accordingly. He is a liaison man, a go-between. And wherever there are workers of some kind extremely alien to industry and to the managers of industry, someone is given this function. He documents, in effect, the gap between the higher positions and the lower; and symbolizes the fact that there is no easy ladder of mobility from the lower position to the higher. He may be literally bilingual, transmitting the orders given in the European tongue into some vernacular; he is also bilingual in a broader figurative sense. He understands the language—the symbols and meanings—of the industrial world, and translates it into symbols which have meaning to people from another culture, who live in a different set of life-chances.

Here we can begin to push harder toward comparison of the mother-countries of industry and the colonial industrial regions. In the latter, the straw-boss symbolizes limited mobility. He is himself mobile and ambitious. But the nature of his job rests on the lack of mobility of the masses. In the mother-countries the straw-boss turns up too. He is found wherever some new and strange element is introduced into the labor force in number. The Negro personnel man is one of the latest straw-bosses; he acts as a liaison between management and Negro help. He cannot himself be considered a candidate for any higher position or for any line position in industry; his is a staff position which exists only so long as Negroes are hired in fairly large numbers, and so long as Negro help is considered sufficiently different from other help to require special liaison. If the race line disappeared, there would be no need of the Negro personnel man. There might then be personnel men who are Negroes. Thus, the Negro personnel man performs a racial function; he is not part of the regular line of authority, and does not represent a rung in the ladder of regular advancement to higher positions. Industrial organizations in the colonial regions abound in such liaison positions. Just what such positions are, the features of social and industrial organization which they reflect, and the kinds of persons who fill them, are all matters whose further analysis would throw light on the nature and internal functioning of industrial organization. It is but one of the several features which appear in clear form in colonial industry, but which may also exist, although commonly overlooked, in the industry of the mother-countries.

Industry in the Western world promoted an ideology of mobility; that is, of ambition. In the colonial world ambition is often regarded as unjustified and dangerous. Even in the Western world managers speak with nostalgia of the unambitious first generation of Poles, French Canadians, or peasant workers of other ethnic groups; people who were content with their jobs, willing to work hard without hope of advancement. Of course, such people often had objectives outside industry to keep them at work and content; notably, the desire to save money for buying property. In spirit they were not completely industrialized. A second or later generation which insists on advancement within industry is compared unfavorably with their fathers. The hostile reaction of many managers to ambitious Negroes is too well-known to require documenting.

Here is apparently a contradiction: Industry encourages

ambition, and complains a good deal about lack of it. On the other hand, it praises some people for not having it, and complains of others who do. Just how much ambition does an industrial organization want, and in how many people, and in what kinds of people does it want it? In the colonial world there is generally a limit on the possibilities of promotion for persons of each ethnic category, although this may change through time. For certain kinds of work it may actually be to the advantage of industry to hire only people whose ambitions are directed to goals completely outside the industrial system. For others they may want ambitious people. There may, however, be some balance between the proportion of ambitious and unambitious people which works best even in the oldest of the industrial regions. A clue appears in a phrase current in a large concern in this country. They have a breed known as the "Thank God for" people; the unambitious people who can be counted on to stay where they are, and who keep things running while others are busy climbing the mobility ladder from one job to another. Analysis might show that in the mother-countries of industry some adjustment between symbol and reality has occurred, so that a large proportion of workers may give lip-service to the mobility ideal, but not too many take it seriously.

Just what proportion of ambitious workers industrial organizations of various kinds can tolerate is a question which merits comparative analysis, although it may be difficult to make the necessary observations in a society where people generally claim to believe in ambition and to be ashamed of lack of it. In colonial regions the talk on the subject is often franker.

We have already noted that ethnic exclusiveness tends to develop at all levels of colonial industrial hierarchies. The dominant managerial and technical functions remain pretty much in the hands of the founding ethnic group. Sometimes a European group of skilled workers, as in South African mines, holds to its level of jobs and succeeds in excluding the natives. In the less skilled jobs, some group of natives may manage to keep out others. Even in American industry such a tendency shows clearly. A number of forces apparently play upon hiring and selection to reinforce or to break up this tendency. If we were to venture an hypothesis it would be something like this: the tendency to exclusiveness is present in all organizations, and in the segments thereof, but the power to maintain it varies. In industry the necessity of keeping a full labor force operates against exclusiveness in those categories where large numbers are required; generally, the lower levels of skill. The people at these levels have little or no formal power of hiring. They have, in varying degree, informal power of selection and rejection. "He is a foreman, although not Irish," furnished the ground for a threatened walk-out in a New England factory which, according to Orvis Collins, management averted by promptly making a new promotion which, this time, was in accord with the ethnic expectations of the men.[11]

The people in the higher levels of the hierarchy have the power to keep their own ranks ethnically exclusive. In the colonial or semi-colonial industrial regions, management often quite frankly talks of the necessity of keeping management in loyal hands; that is, in the hands of people closely identified with one another by national sentiment as well as by general cultural background. In the mother-countries of industry one does not hear such talk, but it is possible that the mechanism operates without people being aware of it. It may operate through the mechanism of sponsoring, by which promising young people are picked and encouraged in their mobility efforts by their superiors. In the course of their rise they are not merely given a technical training, but also are initiated into the ways and sentiments of the managerial group and are judged by their internal acceptance of them. Ethnic, national, and class loyalty are undoubtedly factors in the original choice of people to be sponsored and in their later rise. In the Western world individuals ethnically different from those at the top of management may

---

11. Cf. his "Ethnic Behavior in Industry: Sponsorship and Rejection in a New England Factory," *American Journal of Sociology,* LI (January, 1946), 293-98.

be drawn into the sponsorship circle, but if so, they may effectively lose all symbols of identification with the ethnic group from which they have come and take on those of the receiving group. Where skin color and other racial features are involved this is not so easy to do. Thus, while modern industry is opposed to nepotism, as contrary to the choice of the best people in an open market, as an operating organization it tends to hold power in the hands of a group whose new members are picked from among people thought to be loyal not merely to the particular organization but to the management class and its culture. In the selection and sponsoring process ethnic background plays a large part.

The sponsoring power of lower ranks may be less, but in many situations is by no means completely lacking. Coal miners and railroad workers notoriously have great sponsoring power. And even in the colonial regions the members of an ethnic group or clan, or the inhabitants of a village, may have, in effect, the power to recruit new workers. In a sense, when industry brings in some new ethnic group it has to do it in opposition to the present workers. The actual ethnic composition and changes therein seem then to be a resultant of the operation of demand for new help against the exclusive tendencies of the various segments of the existing working organization. The search of modern industry for new help that can be used with profit has certainly been active and persistent. On the other hand, for a given kind or level of job, the field in which the search is made may be limited by management's own state of knowledge and sentiments. Certainly the evidence is clear that in the colonial regions, and to some extent in the mother-countries, there grows up a body of belief about the special working qualities of various ethnic groups. These stereotypes, which may or may not correspond to the facts, act to limit the vision of those who select help and who initiate sponsorship. In a sense, this is like any marketing situation, in that the bargaining of the marketer is limited by his own knowledge and sentiments. The role of sentiments is, however, made somewhat stronger in the hiring and utilization of human labor than in the buying and selling of inanimate commodities by the fact that the human labor is, so to speak, consumed by industry. Industry is not a labor broker, for it uses the labor to build a continuing organization for work; it must live with its laboring people. And in the course of working together the social and political processes get under way as they do in any organization. Industry thus considers its people not merely as technical help, but as actual or potential participants in a struggle for power within industry and society, and as potential close colleagues (or as unfit to be such). When one takes these points into account, many of the contradictions and paradoxes in the behavior of industrial management and workers begin to move toward possible solution. A complete resolution of them might be approached by systematic comparison of the various situations in which industry has operated. In such a comparison racial and ethnic differences will act as a sort of litmus paper to bring out characteristics and processes which might otherwise be overlooked.

Chapter Six

How They Work for Each Other

Nearly all of the new people in our industrial labor force have had to make some other adjustments at the very time when they were learning a new way of working. They often had to learn to speak a new language, to eat new food, wear new kinds of clothing, live in new kinds of houses, even to meet sickness—sometimes itself of alien types—and death in strange ways. Our immigrant literature is full of the little tragedies of people who in order to survive in America had not only to do work which did not fit their notion of themselves, but to change other ways dear to them. The eastern European rabbi had to go to work with a needle and thread; he, the learned man! And, to add to his humiliation, he was told that it was dangerous to wear his beard and kaftan among powerbelts and high speed sewing machines. But our concern is not with the small personal tragedies so much as with the larger fate of these people in the American division of labor.

For a long time the mass of new labor for North America consisted of European peasants. The French Canadians were an exception only in that they did not come from Europe to New England. They had set up in Canada the closest North

American approximation to a European peasant society. When they began to furnish a large proportion of the hands for New England factories, they were as alien as greenhorns off a ship from Europe.

Only much later, when the European peasant stream was dammed by wars and immigration laws, did our manufacturing industries begin to draw heavily on people already in America but racially or culturally very different from those already in industry: Southern rural Negroes, Mexicans, Chinese, and Japanese, and—though it may sound odd to put them here—old-stock white Southern rural people. For by the time white rural Southerners began to turn up in great numbers in the Northern industrial labor force, the ranks between them and the higher managers had been filled with the children and grandchildren of European peasants. The white Anglo-Saxon Southerner and his boss of Polish extraction were as strange to one another as the Yankee foreman and the Italian laborer had been a couple of generations ago. There are great differences, no doubt, in the course of the adjustment of these various peoples to industrial life, but there are also some common lines.

Immigrants are not generally a cross-section of the people of their home country. Most of the immigrants who came to fill the ranks of labor were peasants, but peasants who had no place on the land. As Handlin has put it,[1] the peasants came to America only when even to stay at home meant change. It is probably not so much poverty, for there are kinds of poverty in which one may be secure, but uprootedness, being without any place in the home economy, that moves people in masses from Europe. This was certainly the story, too, of the French-Canadian farm boy who, if he happened not to be the inheriting son, was compelled to leave the family farm and, as we have seen, find employment in industry.

There were, of course, many immigrant artisans who were

---

1. Oscar Handlin, *The Uprooted* (Boston: Little, Brown and Co., 1951), p. 24.

able to use their skills here. But it was more common to have to enter at the point where least skill was required, since the skills of the peasant are not those of machine industry. The European peasant believed in thrift, in hard work, and in the accumulation of small savings. And however much he had been used to working with kin and friends to whose opinions he would be sensitive, here his tendency was not to pay much attention to the opinions of ethnically alien fellow workers. He seemed, in the new setting, individualistic: at least, he was not eager to join a union. These attitudes the employer often liked, and regretted their disappearance in a second generation. The transplanted peasants seemed to want nothing from their jobs but the money. Their children often wanted a lot of other things—the good opinion of their companions, prestige, a white collar job, a higher standard of living.

As a general rule the peasants who joined the American industrial labor force were not accompanied by middle-class people from their own country. Perhaps a few priests came to save their souls in their own peculiar way. Even when the immigrants were Catholic they wanted priests of their own vernacular; it is well enough to have the Mass in a universal language, but people prefer to confess their sins in the language in which they conceived and committed them. This was but one of many wants so peculiar to their own culture that they could not be met by American professional people and institutions. Indeed, a culture is, seen from one angle, a peculiar set of consumers' wants; and perhaps when people want nothing that cannot be easily supplied by strangers they have no peculiar culture left. Jews want special food, rabbis to circumcise their infant boys, and to teach them things Jewish. Immigrant Sicilians want special food, maybe a special kind of midwife, and someone to ward off the Evil Eye, as well as priests who appreciate their favorite saints and ways of celebrating great days.

Besides these traditional wants of spirit and body which strangers cannot supply there are others which are new; the wants that arise from the very fact of being so far from home. At home one is surrounded by kin who will look after one in sickness and death. Here some substitute for kin and village must be found; so in the new land burial and sickness insurance societies burgeon. Things that seemed to get done without conscious effort in the peasant village here require thought, enterprise, and an organization got up for the purpose.

There was paper work to be done. Letters had to be written home; money saved and sent home to support parents, or to bring wife, fiancée, or kinsman to America. Passports and steamship tickets had to be got to people in the Old Country. It was said cynically in the old Russian empire that you could tell a peasant from a pig because he had a soul and a passport. But the passport wasn't for him to read; it was just to show when he went on journeys or when the Tsar's officers came to see who had done military service and who had not. The New World required more paper work. A Mexican lawyer on Halsted Street in Chicago still includes letter-writing and the reading of government notices among his services to immigrant clients.

In addition to the need for such paper work there is the desire for news. The immigrant could not read the big American newspapers; they did not tell anything about his own people, either here or at home, anyway. So he was ready to spell out what a little newspaper in his own language had to say about the things that really interested him.[2]

Some among the immigrants began to satisfy, each for their own people, these two kinds of peculiar wants, the traditional ones and the ones created by being away from home. The list of special services is surprisingly alike in the varied groups: food, clothing (but not for long as they must and soon do take up the clothing of their new country and their new work), religion, medicine—both folk and professional—paper work, insurance, and other devices to meet crises,

---

2. Robert E. Park, *The Immigrant Press and Its Control* (New York: Harper and Bros., 1922).

news, sociability, preservation of home traditions, and protection against the exigencies of the new life.

Since professional and business people from home did not not come hither in any number, the supplying of these many wants was undertaken by peasant immigrants themselves. Thus there grew up a complement of service institutions. They furnished opportunity for a few of the group to rise in the new world on the backs of their fellows. Italians imported and sold to their compatriots spaghetti, olives, olive oil; they grew zucchini and broccoli to sell to them. Some then sold them to others. Irishmen learned to corral votes and trade them for jobs on city streets, and in city ditches and later in city hall offices, handling papers, or on the police force. Bohemians and Poles want to buy houses; men of their own group founded savings and loan banks and real estate agencies. Other immigrants founded newspapers in their mother tongues, burial and sickness societies, protective associations. Some women served as midwives to fellow peasant women who had never thought of going to male physicians. Some immigrants or immigrants' sons got into the medical profession—although that takes time and money —and found a natural clientele among their own people. In short, the beginnings of a middle class rose by giving services to the immigrants.

In the meantime the mass of the immigrants were at work in the industries or businesses of the greater economy of the country. They mined coal and made steel or clothing, not for their own kind, but for all. Most groups tended to concentrate in one or a few industries, and at the bottom thereof; it is certainly not the rule for immigrants to be distributed as by chance among the industries of a country. Slavs were concentrated in heavier industry; Jews in the needle trades; Italians started mainly on construction work, as had the Irish. Sometimes people got into an industry for which they had some tradition. The Italians, indeed, are an example. They have known how to pave roads for many a century. Often the Italian straw-boss of a road gang in this country went on up in the world to become a paving contractor, learning enough about politics to know how to get the contracts. At the depth of the depression of the 30's, when French Canada had plenty of excess labor, Italians as always were paving the streets of Montreal. The French complained of it, but it went on just the same. Many ethnic groups have risen by the practice of some traditional skill or trade.

Generally, however, the concentration of an immigrant group in an industry seems to have nothing to do with previous occupation. It appears to be a matter of labor needs when they arrive, physique, and perhaps many subtler features of their culture or situation. Once in a given industry, and at the bottom of it, members of a group may spread in two directions: upward in the industries or occupational hierarchies in which they started; and outward into other industries and occupations. A group may feel cramped and discriminated against in both these dimensions. They may believe—and be right—that people of other ethnic groups both prevent their rise and their spread into other kinds of work. And the second is as crucial as the first, for if a group is to find a good place in the economic structure it must have access to the bottom rungs of several ladders.

Our main economic structure of business and industry is supposed to be a ladder of mobility up which one may climb step by step from the very bottom. But it appears that the number of steps one may climb from the bottom is becoming fewer and fewer. One rises generally by learning to do things he could not do before. Such things may be learned either by experience in industry, or by training got outside industry. Training got outside is, in turn, of two kinds: that which gives one skills such as reading slide-rules, calculating stresses and strains, testing samples or keeping accounts; and that which gives one a license, or mandate, to do something. The latter gives one a "right" to try; it makes one a legitimate candidate for a job. The tendency in industry now is to require of candidates for higher positions more and more of the training got outside: an engineering degree has become the necessary license to try to be an engineer. Some industries hire college-graduated trainees with or without the specific understanding that if they do not qualify for supervisory positions within a certain time they must get out. Some union contracts provide that a man who moves up to foremanship cannot be bumped back into the crew. There is thus apt to be a sharp line above which one can scarcely rise without a good deal of the kind of training that is got outside—that is, in schools and colleges. The fate of a group coming up from the bottom depends thus not only on its access to that knowledge which is gained on the job, but on how far its children get in the educational system outside, and especially in those parts of it which make one a legitimate candidate for higher positions.

Whether the children of an ethnic group will get such higher education depends somewhat on the economic achievement of the parents. Poor boys go to college, but not so many of them as better-off boys; and the very poorest rarely go. It depends also upon the goals of ambition current in the group, or upon those accessible as models to the young people. Those who have no education often know neither what kinds of education are necessary for various careers, nor how one would go about getting them. People vary not merely as to their level of ambition, but as to their knowledge and perception of the positions available and of the means of attaining them. It requires some sophistication and social skill for a person to climb into a position in which he can learn what is necessary for climbing still higher.

A good deal of promotion in industry turns around the selection of people who can make not merely one step upward, but who can keep on going up. The selection of people for such promotion is a kind of sponsoring. And here members of groups which have hitherto been only in the lower positions have a special problem. How do they get themselves even considered as candidates? For those who have sponsoring power are rarely indifferent to ethnic identity. They may consciously believe that ethnic groups already most represented at higher levels are inherently fitter for them, and that the groups at the bottom are there because of lack of ability or ambition. Or they may simply, all unconsciously, wear blinders which limit their field of vision to people of their own kind.

At any rate, the problem of the group which is starting—as do most immigrant groups—at the bottom and in a few kinds of industry, is both to rise and to spread toward a job distribution approaching that of other elements of the population. The group's own standard of living, conceptions of occupational goals and knowledge of attaining them, will interact with conditions of the market and the degree and kinds of discrimination against them to determine their progress in the main economic structure. The same factors, of course, operate when Negroes or other ethnic minorities already in the country are drawn into industry, and when industry invades a country and uses a native labor force—as in French Canada, parts of South America, and many other regions. We have commented in a previous chapter on some of the difficulties met in rising in the hierarchy of industry.

Now, let us remember that these people are the customers and clients of those who constitute the service structure of the immigrant or minority group. The fate of the middle class which grows up by catering to their peculiar wants is dependent upon the fate of the group in the main economic structure. If the group as a whole continues to have a very low standard of living, a middle class serving it and it only cannot rise and expand very far. The middle class may for this reason, as well as from a sense of identity with their group and from a desire for justice for all, want the group to progress to ever better jobs, incomes, and ever higher standards of living. But their position breeds ambivalence. For as the group gets better off (more widely distributed as to jobs, income, education, and styles of consumption), they may lose the peculiar wants to which their own middle class has been catering. Some Italians may no longer care whether the priest who confesses them is Italian; their children may, in fact, want to go to the "American" parish; that is, the older one established by the Irish that is found in most towns which have several Catholic parishes. Women may respond to advertising and begin to buy standard brands of groceries from chain stores. Some people may find that there is more prestige in going to physicians not of their own ethnic group; or else they come to want specialized services which physicians of their own kind do not offer. The very progress of the group in the main economic and social system may weaken the monopoly of the ethnic service group over the custom of their own people. Hence the not infrequent accusation by people of a minority that their own middle-class leaders have a vested interest in segregation; for behind the wall they can build up a monopoly.

Whether the middle class will enjoy a monopoly of the business and professional patronage of its own ethnic group will depend upon several circumstances. The want served may be peculiar to the culture: the Chinese in America wanted soy sauce when no one else did. Or the need may not be peculiar but the people may not want it filled by strangers: most people like to have their dead buried by their own kind. Only a Jew can undertake the ritual slaughtering and inspecting necessary if meat is to be kosher.

There is also the opposite case of monopoly in which ritual taboos of certain activities make it necessary to have outsiders perform them. Strict Jews, for example, have often had to have housework done by Gentiles in order that they themselves might refrain from forbidden activities on holy days. For a long time Christians had to leave banking to Jews because of a religious taboo. The taboos of the in-group may turn a monopoly of the dirty work over to strangers. We will speak of that later.

It also happens that those who dispense some services to the population at large may not bother or want to dispense them to certain ethnic or racial groups. The grocer who finds his neighborhood filled with ethnic strangers may simply not try to adapt his stock to their wants. The professional man may not try to understand the terms in which new people describe symptoms and troubles, and the peculiar things which distress them. The business or professional man who serves people of older ethnic elements may positively not

want the newcomers or minority people as clients either because of his own prejudices or because of fear of losing his
present clients. White physicians who, in our Northern
states, have or hope to have an upper middle-class clientele
are made unhappy by the sight of poorly dressed or colored
people in their waiting rooms. They, like barbers, hotel
keepers, and others, are afraid the most desired customers or
clients will run away if they see such people being served.
Business and professional people measure their success in
part by the kinds of people whom they serve. Most Chicago
school teachers seek to flee from the slums to those schools
where they can teach children from "nice families." Many
white teachers think they have to explain away the fact of
teaching Negro children.

On the other hand, clients may prefer to receive goods
and services from people of some rather than of other ethnic,
class, and religious groups, and from one sex rather than the
other. Miss Josephine Williams found this so of medical
services in a middle-class Chicago neighborhood; preferences
were stronger with respect to some specialties than others.[3]
Many people also prefer to buy their clothes, and to have it
known that they do, from the same stores as do their social
betters whose peers they would like to be. The same applies
to other services, such as sermons, wedding ceremonies, medical attention, and hair curling.

The attitudes known as prejudice, and the actions called
discrimination, then, will enter into the actual balance between monopoly and competition. The balance may alter,
as groups continue to live in contact with one another,
which is one of many contingencies affecting the fate of the
ethnic or racial minority service structure. The group might
lose peculiar wants and its preference for getting services
even of an intimate kind from ethnic fellows. The minority
middle class would then lose its monopoly. At the same time
various professions might cease to draw lines in selecting
people for training and colleagueship. The population at

---

3. Josephine J. Williams, "Patients and Prejudice," *American Journal of
Sociology*, LI, No. 4 (January, 1946), pp. 283-87.

large might also lose its preference for getting services from their own ethnic kind, and might specifically cease to be prejudiced against the professionals of newer ethnic groups. In this ideal case—approaching free competition—the people in the minority service structure could move into the main or dominant service structure of the community. But the changes necessary to bring it about ordinarily do not all happen at the same rates.

The instances we have been discussing are chiefly those to be found in the ethnically-mixed community, where a particular culture gives a particular value to a commodity or service. Since culture is virtually identical among American Negroes and American whites, the racially-mixed community in our country exhibits more nearly, perhaps, than anywhere else in the world the pure case of the sorting out of customers and clients along *caste* lines. In the South there are perhaps a few services wanted by Negroes because of ways in which their tastes differ from those of white people; that is, because of cultural differences. But class for class, these differences are slight. Many of the peculiar services which Negroes of a certain class can offer, such as love potions, are also wanted by whites. But in the main any peculiarities of service wanted by Negroes in this country are a result of a difference of condition and of position in society. If they want their hair straightened instead of curled, or their skin lightened instead of darkened by sun-lamp and beach tanning, it is that they may be more, not less, like other people. Negroes in the North want, at least for a time and like other Southerners, some regional foods—crackling, greens and hominy grits. Some Negroes build small businesses on these and other minor peculiar wants of Negro migrants from the South. In the main, however, the Negro middle class, to repeat, is founded not on peculiar wants, but on the color-caste line. Culture, it is true, enters in to the extent that the forms of monopoly and competition themselves became encysted in the culture. But the point remains that the discrimination is against not the commodity or the service but against the person dispensing it. In this sense, we have a pure case of prejudice and discrimination.

Consider, for example, a hypothetical community with both white and Negro doctors serving one hundred patients, half of whom are Negro, half white. There will be a considerable variety of *theoretically possible* combinations of custom or patronage. In reviewing the possible combinations of patients and physicians our purpose is not so much to classify actual conditions that may be found here or there among us and elsewhere on the earth, but to bring to our attention all possibilities, including those we might otherwise overlook because, in our eyes, they are too preposterous for serious consideration.

In the first place, there might be *complete segregation*: the doctors of each race have the monopoly of practice among their own people, Negroes going to doctors of their own race and whites to doctors of theirs. But segregation could conceivably take contrary form: all white patients might go to Negro doctors only, while all Negro patients go to white doctors only.

There is also *complete dominance*: The Negro physicians have all the patients, regardless of race; or the white physicians have them all.

There are four possible situations of *partial dominance*. In all four, doctors of each race have some share in patients of the other race. But in one case the white doctors have also the monopoly of white patients (this, in general, is the state of affairs in American cities). In a second case the white doctors monopolize all the Negro patients, as well as having a share of the whites. The third and fourth possibilities are the corresponding situations, as regards the Negro physicians; they treat patients of both races, but enjoy also a monopoly over, in one case, the white; in the other case, the Negro sick.

Finally, there is the situation of indifference and full competition. Now the patients go in pure chance proportions to doctors of the two races. That this is a thing we have never seen renders it no less important as a conception. At least, we may suppose that in Brazil the situation is somewhat closer to it than in South Africa or North America.

Now let us pass from these abstract constructions to the realities.

The Negro in the middle-class service structure has never had a monopoly of trade or practice among his own people except where the white service structure refuses to accept the Negro client. This is the case with barbering and beauty care in the North now; but not many years ago Negro barbers had access to both races. And he may have none but Negro clients, because the whites will not accept his services. White men in the North do not as a rule want to bury Negro dead, treat Negro sick, or preach or perform marriages for Negroes. Undertaking, medicine, and the ministry, then, are areas in which Negroes have some measure of monopoly of their own people.

White professional and business men have often not given Negroes access to their services. Public and private educational institutions dominated by whites have made it difficult for even those Negroes who could afford higher training to get it. Some combination of colleague and patient prejudice keeps the Negro physician from most of the internships and residencies required for specialty training. Even if Negroes were acceptable to white patients, it is doubtful whether the white physician would refer patients to them—and referral is the heart of the medical system in this age of specializing. Occasionally a Negro physician may be known as a wonder-worker, to whom patients of all races and conditions make pilgrimages from afar. But it is not referral by family physician that sends them to such men; it is other patients who have had wonders done for them.

The Negro monopoly in medicine has never been complete. In the South the Negro physician has access only to Negroes, while white physicians may have both white and Negro patients—one of the patterns of partial dominance. A white physician may, indeed, have a monopoly over the practice of medicine among the Negro tenants who are dependent upon a white plantation owner for credit. The owner picks the doctor. Sometimes there is no Negro physician within reach of rural people, and the white doctor may have all medical practice entirely in his hands. In cities it is common for the Negro physicians not to have access to the few Negro wards and clinics of white-dominated hospitals.

In the North, Negro physicians may come closer to a monopoly of Negro patients, but there are still white physicians who have a good deal of Negro practice. The most violent anti-Negro talk we ever heard came from a white graduate of a famous medical school who, instead of achieving a good upper-middle class white practice, finds himself practicing over a drugstore in a run-down Negro area. He treats people who get knifed in Saturday-night fights, and examines on behalf of insurance companies people who claim to have been injured in falling off street cars. His low-class Negro patients are the symbol of his failure; he hates them. But he would hate low-class white patients if he had them. The white physician may treat Negroes because he can get no other patients; or he may do so because, as a successful specialist, he gives of his time to Negro patients in a clinic. But the Negro physician can have the bulk of Negro practice so long as his patients do not need to go to hospitals.

The Negro lawyer gets practically no white practice, and far from all of the Negro practice. The white lawyer enjoys partial dominance, having all the white practice and a share of Negro clients. Mr. William Hale [4] found that a white lawyer often gets the cases of poor Negroes, rarely of the Negro middle class. To the poor, the law is trouble to be got out of. A lower-class Negro wants to win an insurance case against a utility or an employer. A Negro woman has a son in jail and wants to get him out. They often believe that a white lawyer can manipulate all these institutions better than a Negro lawyer could: it is, after all, a white man's world. They may get the white lawyer through a store-front preacher or a ward-heeler of their own race. On the other hand,

---

4. William H. Hale, "The Career Development of the Negro Lawyer in Chicago" (Unpublished Ph.D. thesis, Department of Sociology, University of Chicago, September, 1949).

the middle-class Negro wants a divorce which has already been agreed upon; he wants a deed, articles of partnership or incorporation, or advice concerning a contract. It is "friendly" law. He goes to the Negro lawyer and feels very loyal to his race. He and the lawyer are both part of that relatively small group, successful middle-class Negroes who got there by serving Negroes.

Negro lawyers might, then, improve their position in one or more of several ways. They could get more firmly into politics and get a bigger share in the power of manipulating things in favor of clients in that kind of trouble. They might work toward general improvement in the standard of living of the Negro population, so that fewer would be in trouble with the law and more would have "friendly" law work. Or they might get access to white clients and thus enter into the main stream of competition for law work of all kinds. [5]

All things which affect the measure of monopoly which the professional and business people have over the custom of their own and/or other kinds of people set the fateful career problems of the minority middle-class person. The drama thus is played in terms of crucial and painful decisions. As Oswald Hall has shown, [6] the Italian doctor in a certain New England city may have security and a moderate income if he is content with a general practice among his Italian kin and neighbors. He will, of course, be known as an Italian doctor, and will not have much prestige among the fraternity of successful specialists who dominate the hospitals and the referral system. Should he, however, try to establish himself as a specialist and to break away from Italian practice, he may fall between two stools. He may fail

---

5. Some years ago we discovered through an inquiry undertaken with Mr. Stuart Jamieson that French lawyers in Montreal were much more in small family firms than the English lawyers. The latter are concentrated in a very few firms who work for the larger Canadian companies. The French people are in small businesses, and evidently the French lawyer concentrates on that kind of practice.

6. "The Informal Organization of Medical Practice in an American City" (Unpublished Ph.D. dissertation, Department of Sociology, University of Chicago, 1944).

to get a firm enough footing in the general sponsorship and referral system to allow him to go ahead without a core of Italian practice. Moreover, in the course of trying to get started in the big medical world, he may alienate both his Italian colleagues and his Italian potential patients. Like other ambitious persons in a racial or ethnic minority he must decide whether to stake his career on the possibility of getting clean out of his group into the larger general competition in his business or profession—with a higher ceiling of possible success, and a deeper pit of failure to fall into—or to let his group-identity determine his career-fate, to let its ceiling be his ceiling. The choice is not always his. It may be made for him by the denial of colleagueship and the exclusion from customers or clients outside his group. But there comes to be some area of freedom in the choice in many ethnic groups; indeed, in this country many of them are in that phase now.

Sometimes the choice is complicated by a willingness of professionals and clients of the more dominant groups to delegate dirty work to professionals of a minority. Law firms of great respectability sometimes remain so by referring the shadier parts of their clients' work to other lawyers, often of other ethnic groups. In these cases the minority professional is given access to clients not of his group; indeed, to clients of the kind most desired by the profession at large, but on conditions that prevent later entry into the dominant brotherhood of the successful. There may arise something of a division of respectable and disreputable labor between ethnic groups within a business or profession. The competitive area of the minority group may be thereby broadened, but its ceiling lowered.

Related to the decision whether to try to practice or do business among one's own is the choice of occupations itself. The young Negro in this country may run the chance of training for an occupation for which there are no Negro employers or customers, in the hope that the battle against segregation will proceed rapidly enough to allow him to find a job or clients without regard to race. Architects, engineers, and chemists have not had much place in the ethnic service structure of Negroes or of other ethnic groups: their services are as a rule wanted and bought only by representatives of the main economic institutions of the country. The young Negro may gamble on the walls of Jericho falling for him; but he also runs the chance of getting a sore head from too much bumping. It is his fate to have to make the choice.

Chapter Seven

Status and Identity

That a Negro American is fated to have to make choices that other people do not have to make is evidence that he has a peculiar status or standing. To be declared a Negro by one's fellow Americans is to be assigned to a category of people whose privileges and duties are different from those of people not declared Negro; the contingencies of life, the one life a man has to live, are different because he is of that category. That is social fate, and it is social status. A society also has a fate; sometimes its fate is to be changed by people who do not like the way in which justice and opportunities are distributed, that is, the system of status.

We have here used the historic and generic meaning of status: "the standing or position of a person as determined by his membership of some class of persons legally enjoying certain rights or subject to certain limitations." [1] In all societies, individuals are classified, and thereby differentiated as to social fate. Some of the categories are easy to escape from; others are not. People of some categories have more

---

1. *Shorter Oxford Dictionary*. Station, standing, estate, and the French *état* and German *Stand* are of the same derivation and carry similar meanings. All tend to be extended to include the notion of *high* standing, hence of ranked status. They also tend to get political meaning, since the constitution of a state—again considered in its generic meaning—is the manner in which political participation and power are distributed among the estates.

power and are treated with greater deference than those of others; status connotes rank. Indeed, the pregnant meaning (as the dictionary calls it) of rank appears to be displacing the generic meaning of the word *status*. Perhaps this connotation is the reason why so many Americans, including social scientists, object to talk of status altogether. It suggests there may be social ranking in America. [2]

Questions of status are the heart of racial and ethnic relations; those relations, indeed, can scarcely be said to exist if there is no question of status. One cannot, in the sociological sense, even say that a society contains diverse racial groups unless they are defined as status categories.

In the course of history some characteristics become the basis of status; others do not. It would require some stretching of the facts to say that there is a social group of red-headed or left-handed people in this country, though theoretically there could be. But, as it happens, we have no laws or customs which differentiate them from other people. There are a few sayings, and enough special talk, to make the red-headed person conscious of being one. Perhaps it becomes thus a part of his personality. The left-handed individual has been somewhat more the object of special definition and controls; it used to take a strong-willed parent to defeat the school's attempt to make all pupils right-handed. However, the social differentiation is weak in both these cases; red-heads and "south-paws" have no status, as such. But if society did make these characteristics the basis of special disabilities, they would not be argued out of existence by declaring that there is no difference between red-heads and "south-paws" and other people. For other

---

2. Some of the objection shows a peculiar inversion common in American sociology. Cooley noted that in Western society contractual relations—made willingly and for a special purpose and fixed term—tend to replace those of status, i.e., of obligations based on assignment of individuals to enduring social categories. Maine, Toennies, and others have written in the same vein. Cooley's statement is repeatedly turned into an assertion that there is no status in our society. The allegation of fact then becomes an ethical dictum: "We should not have status in our society; and anyone who says we do is reactionary."

people would have a sharp eye for these characteristics and would associate them with the imputed differences. There might come a time when a person's social fate would no longer depend upon his red hair or left-handedness. Then no one would bother to mention it unless some special circumstance made it of interest.

All societies emphasize some series of individual characteristics and assign people social identities accordingly. A good deal of each person's inner drama is discovery of the identity given him by others and his reactions to it and to the people who define him so. He may accept eagerly and even exploit the identifications people are inclined to give him. He may reject them and try to establish others. He may join a movement to change social definitions, for the characteristics by which assignment to social identities are made do change. One can hardly imagine a more drastic change, for it involves this question: What must I know about a person to know how I should act toward him, to predict how he will behave, and to keep our relationship such that neither of us will get into trouble with others?

Whenever two peoples live in the same community their systems of classifying people, that is, their systems of status, become entangled in some measure. At first the two peoples are distant from or, at least, external to each other. Each has its own internal system of differences and identifications, its answers to the questions "Who am I?" and "Who is that?" The two systems are external to each other in two respects: subjectively, in that an individual in either society does not know or care what individuals in the other society think of him; objectively, in that it does not matter, since one has crucial relationships only with members of his own society. Thus the important thing for the individual is to be known and socially identified by his own people.

But with contact, and in varying degree in different kinds of contact, the two societies are no longer so completely external to each other. Some people of society A become sensitive to the social judgments of some in society B. In time each group, more or less as a communicating whole, gets a standard definition of the other. Then they cease to be two separate status systems and become parts of a new one that embraces both groups. Then arises the question: Which of the two groups will have the greater power in defining the relationships between them? As the contact continues, there always come to be some individuals who might with some right belong to either group. It is not clear to which they belong. Which of the two groups will claim and get the prerogative of saying where these mixed, ambiguous persons belong?

Sometimes one group is so superordinate that it will appear to have complete power to assign membership and to draw the lines as it wishes. In the United States and in South Africa white people have set the tests for determining who is white and who is Negro, for purposes of work, education, marriage, police protection, and Christian worship. In this country the tests are of two kinds: the physical appearance of the individual and his known or imputed ancestry. If a person is white by the test of physical appearance he can "pass" for white—a phrase reminiscent of the good soldier Schwejk's friend who died in a military hospital "simulating tuberculosis"! Negroes who know that some of his ancestors were known as Negroes could betray this fact to white people and so turn the "passing" white man back into a Negro. Negroes may also withdraw in-group protection from an individual, betraying him thus into the hands of the white man. This was done to a "passing" Negro in a Chicago industry. He was overheard acquiescing in anti-Negro talk. The Negro workers did not tell white people that the man was "passing," but surreptitiously put so many faulty pieces of work on his table that he was discharged.

Even where formal definition lies completely in the hands of one group, the other may retain the power to reject anyone from the informal we-group or in-group. But there are no mechanisms in the United States for complete and universal rejection of a man from the Negro race; there are such for turning some white men irrevocably into Negroes.

The long British political domination in India, even when buttressed by the social snobbishness of embattled British wives of colonial officials and army officers, never touched the power of castes to accept and reject whom they would—including the British conquerors. The local council of a caste determines who, in the given locality, may join them in ritual and who are acceptable marriage partners. A person rejected by what he would like to consider his own caste is not thereby made a member of any other. And so, where each group can reject individuals, one may expect a multiplication of mutually exclusive groups, with a tendency for every new in-between group to become a new status. This is apparently what happened in India.

There might have been just such an array of exclusive groups in this country if the power of classifying had not been so completely monopolized by the whites. Here and there small groups for a time do succeed to some degree in maintaining a precarious status between Negro and white. Mr. Vernon Parenton of Louisiana State University and Mr. Joseph Hardy Jones, Jr., who have lately been studying small communities [3] of light-colored people in their state, find that they are, in fact, extended kin groups which are very exclusive. They hope not to fall into the general category of Negro. The free Negroes of the south-eastern states tried to maintain themselves in similar fashion before the Civil War. There was every motive for any group which could possibly do so to keep free of the disabilities of the status of Negro. An exclusive extended kin group, ejecting those who marry unacceptable partners, is an incipient caste. The white population, however, has always had the power to check proliferation of such groups by enforcing its simpler classification of the population into two racial categories.

The nature of these two American racial statuses illustrates another distinction. One of the races is defined in an exclusive, the other in a residual or inclusive, fashion. The white race is defined strictly; all doubtful cases are in effect thrown

---

3. "The People of Frilot Cove; A Study of Racial Hybrids," *American Journal of Sociology,* LVII, no. 2 (Sept. 1951), pp. 145-9.

into the Negro category. This does not mean that the people in the exclusively defined group are necessarily alike in many respects. The white group in this country, which has received new recruits from the countries of Europe throughout our history, is of greater cultural variety than the Negro Americans, nearly all of whom are of older American stock. In most northern cities the areas with the highest proportion of people born of native American parents and with English surnames are the Negro districts.

In Canada the French Canadians are the exclusive group. One is a French Canadian only by descent. But in this case the group is also homogeneous in culture, and especially so in religion. One may be a French-speaking Catholic and have lived his life among French Canadians; but if his paternal grandfather was Irish, he is not quite a French Canadian. The census-taker would probably list him as Irish. On the other hand, when families of pure French-Canadian descent turn Protestant, they are at once outside French-Canadian society. All French Canadians are Catholic; free-thinkers, perhaps, but Catholic, not Protestant. We suspect that French-Canadian culture remains relatively stable because its free-thinkers and its rebels, if too uncomfortable, have a whole continent to escape into, taking their deviant views with them and leaving the culture intact.

There are several ways in which there come to be people of doubtful identity in communities where ethnic groups meet. Some children are born of parents not both of the same race, ethnic group, or religion. These people, one of the kinds to whom Park gave the name "marginal men," may be assigned to the father's group, or to the mother's group, or their position may remain in doubt. Some people on a cultural or racial frontier may simply elect to live as if they were members of the other group, the one they were not born into. They take on the culture of the other group. It may go deeper than a few outward changes, as in the case of a light-colored Negro woman who was a Seventh Day Adventist who came to work for a white family in Chicago. After a few days the gay and attractive black young woman who worked next door made occasion to ask the mistress of the Adventist, in all sincerity, "Is Mary colored? I just can't tell, because she certainly doesn't act like a colored person." Allowing for some spite in the question, it still suggests the power of conversion to a certain kind of sect to change the personality from that expected in one group to that expected in another. Religious conversion often creates ambiguity of group identification. In addition to these extreme cases there are people who—without renunciation of the group they were born into and without doubt having been cast on who they are—take on some of the characteristics of members of the other group. If this happens to members of both groups, the line between them may get blurred in a quite undramatic way.

The course of such blurring may be affected by the direction and strength of the sensitivity of members of each group to the opinions of the other. Undoubtedly Negroes in this country have been more sensitive to the opinions of whites than whites have been to the opinions of Negroes. This is not to say that even the man who believes most firmly in keeping Negroes in their (subordinate) place is never sensitive to what Negroes think of him. Mr. Harry Walker tells the story of a Negro elevator man in a Southern court house who blackmailed lawyers into lending him money by playing on their pride. He would remark to a lawyer going up of a morning how successful and busy he must be; then, while the lawyer was basking in the warm sense of having at least one admirer, that admirer would ask him for five dollars. If the lawyer had been indifferent to the opinion of the elevator man he could have refused the loan. Newly rich families are notoriously sensitive to the opinions of servants who have been the familiars of aristocrats. Even aristocratic white women are not above seeking a Negro servant's opinion of a new neighbor. Lately we have a new group of people sensitive to Negro opinion: white people who feel so guilty about the wrongs done Negroes that they cringe at every accusation, just or not, made by a Negro. But, by and large, Negroes have been more sensitive to white opinion than the reverse. Thus one of the services which Negroes perform for people of their race is to supply them with cream to make skin look lighter, and hot oil treatments to make hair straight—like the skin and hair of white people. Negro newspapers are supported by advertisements of products to make Negroes look more like white people, while the rest of the paper protests that they should be themselves—a familiar kind of contradiction in the press. Of course, one must bear in mind that Negroes have very often found it wise to pretend to greater respect for white opinion than they really feel.

Jews in America, we suspect, have been more sensitive to the opinions of Gentiles than vice versa. Occasionally one hears of a child who wishes he were Jewish and could share the holiday festivities of his Jewish schoolmates. We know well that it is not true that Jews think especially highly of Christians, for the dirtiness and stupidity of the Goyim are common themes of talk and contemptuous jest. In fact, Jews spend millions to reform the Christians; the reform wanted is that the Christians should think better of the Jews. So are the strands of sensitivity to out-group opinions tangled. We may generally expect that when two groups live side by side the currents of sensitivity, imitating, and pretending will run mainly in one direction. There may, however, be unsuspected hidden currents in the other direction.

The relations between peoples of two kinds in the same community may become defined in several ways which we speak of as status systems. We noted several of them in canvassing the racial and cultural frontiers of the world. A common one is the colonial form which occurs when an outside group, small in number, invade a territory and draw the native tribal peoples into the labor force of commercial agricultural and extractive enterprises. The natives, in the measure that they are drawn away from village and tribal life, are *detribalized,* and form a bottom stratum of a new kind of society. The invaders form an upper layer and soon become accustomed to a measure of power and luxury not known to them in their country of origin. The result is a hierarchy of two widely separated ranks, with little or no passage from

one to the other. The lower stratum will tend to be called by
some common group name, such as the term "Natives" in
South Africa. To this extent they get a common identity, no
matter what their own notions of who they are and no matter
what their distinctions. In such cases, the invaders eventually
set up a system of law applying to all who live in or enter a
certain territory, except that the law will not be in all re-
pects the same for the invaders and the natives. Sometimes
the native tribal leaders are allowed to continue to dispense
justice among their own people. But what about quarrels
between people of two tribes, between two natives both of
whom are far from home, living in the white man's compound or city, or between a native and a white man? These
inevitably are decided by the superordinate group. Even in
the cases where natives are tried by their own law it is the
white man who says who is, for the purposes of the law, a
native. If the fiction is maintained, as in certain cases in
South Africa, that a native is subject to the law of his own
tribe, there must be someone who determines—in doubtful
cases—what tribe a man belongs to. Thus native custom and
law become a part of the general legal system dominated by
the invading group. Law, let it be said, may be no respecter of
persons; but it is a creator of status, in that it constantly gives
answers to these questions: Who are these people? Since they
are who they are, what are their rights and obligations to each
other?

One of the most fundamental of all the problems of status
is the question: Who has a right to bring complaints before
the law and against whom? Who, in other words, has a right
to be heard? In the colonial circumstances mentioned it is
usually made much easier for the person of the superordinate
racial rank to complain against the lowly native than the reverse. This is an old problem of social hierarchies, whether
or not they are inter-racial; it is the problem of preserving
equality of recourse to justice where wealth, rank, and power
are not equal. Wherever peoples meet, eventually some pro-
visions will be made for handling those new combinations in
which people may act together, and possibly quarrel. Sup-

pose, in earlier India, a British private soldier clashes with a highly-placed Brahmin; or, in the American south, that a middle-class educated Negro runs afoul of an illiterate white cotton tenant. These cases run counter to the general slope of power and superordination and are probably the most difficult to bring under control.

Even quarrels between members of a single group become different when the group is part of a larger inter-ethnic community. Generally, people will try to settle their in-group quarrels quietly and without recourse to more formal proceedings which may be in the hands of ethnic strangers who do not know or respect the finer points of in-group sentiments of justice. When an ethnic group is in an inferior position, complaint to the law exposes the whole group to danger. He who carries a quarrel to the alien masters is an informer, just as is the prisoner or schoolboy who "squeals" on a mate to guards or teachers. It is not unusual for a private or kangaroo justice to grow up to take care of such cases. The Japanese and the Jewish family in the United States—both acutely sensitive to the opinion of the ethnic majority—make tremendous sacrifices to prevent a black sheep in their midst from becoming a public scandal.

We mentioned just now the kind of status system which arises when tribal peoples become the lower stratum of a colonial society. It never remains a simple affair of two categories. In time the great gap between the two groups may be partially filled by people of mixed ancestry who manage to get a position better than that of the native bottom layer. It may be partly filled by immigrants of some non-tribal people other than that of the dominant invaders. Typically such people come in as traders, or as laborers and soon turn to trade. East Indians and Chinese have done so in many parts of the world where Europeans established empires and enterprises among tribal or village agricultural peoples. Before World War II, in the Outer Provinces of the Netherlands East Indies, a middle stratum of Chinese traders and money lenders numbered thirteen times the European population. Such a gap-filling group is likely to be regarded as outsiders by both the dominant top group and by the subordinate native; indeed, a special body of law may be developed to define their relations with other kinds of people. Weber pointed out that the aristocratic landlord and the peasant in Eastern Germany were united in their hatred of the Jew, the stranger whom they both owed money. Similarly in South Africa, Native and white have united against the East Indian trader; and in Thailand, against the Chinese money lender.

Perhaps there is a special fierceness against the gap-fillers, whether they be alien or not. The in-betweeners may be disliked for an alleged pretentious exclusiveness. The southern free Negroes who had some property in the days of slavery had to be very tightly exclusive to preserve their small advantages. One runaway slave caught in their midst would have threatened the whole group; it was best to admit no new people to their churches and no outsiders to the cemeteries that were the symbol of their independence. To people at the bottom, such in-betweeners are the resented tangible barriers in the way of the first steps upward in the social scale. To those of the top group, especially to those whose personal positions are not secure, the people between ranks may appear as threats to what sour small advantage there is in having status where one is without wealth or personal prestige.

Certainly under modern conditions of money economy such status-gaps do tend to be filled by people who, at least economically, are intermediate between the laborers of one race and the masters of the other. The resulting legal and social definitions of status and the political consequences may vary.

It is in those cases which start with a wide status-gap between the races that one may expect a racial caste system to arise; that is, a set of social and legal definitions which are designed to prevent any member of a lower group from crossing the line into the higher under any circumstances whatsoever.[4]

---

4. The word "caste" is of Latin origin, and passed through Portuguese into English. It meant race or breed and thence, easily, a family or lineage. In 18th century India Portuguese women were called *Castees*. (T. G. P.

The nature of the race-caste line in the United States is sharply indicated by the fact that we do not allow mixed families. Intermarriage is always frowned upon, and in some states is illegal. But interbreeding occurs, with or without marriage. In all such cases the family is assigned to the Negro race. When a couple consisting of a white man and a Negro woman have children the resulting family has traditionally consisted only of the mother and the children. The father was not part of it. It was necessarily a matriarchal family. If, as happens sometimes in the North, the husband is Negro and the wife white, the wife becomes, in effect, Negro with her children. All mixed families are Negro. So strong is this rule that white women who marry Negroes are generally—if their families cannot get them declared insane, as a middle-class family will try to do—read out of their families.

Even so strict a race-caste line has not prevented large numbers of American Negroes from getting educations, manners of living, and occupations much superior to those of many white people. This creates what Warner calls a *status fault*,[5] illustrating it by a diagram in which the whites, in the upper position, are separated from the Negroes, in the lower,

Spear, *The Nabobs, a Study of the Social Life of the English in Eighteenth Century India* [London: Oxford University Press, 1932]). Evidently the Portuguese applied this word to the exclusive groups in India and the term was adopted in other European languages. George W. Cable, writing his *Old Creole Days* (New York: Charles Scribner's Sons, 1926), in the 1870's spoke repeatedly of the "free quadroon caste" which existed in New Orleans in the early 19th century. Here the reference was to an exclusive, in-between group which had something of the nature of an Indian caste. Students of race relations have generally used *caste* to refer to the racial groups in this country and their meaning was quite clear. (Cf. Robert E. Park, *Race and Culture*, "The Bases of Race Prejudice" (Glencoe, Illinois: The Free Press, 1950), pp. 230-43; W. L. Warner, "American Class and Caste," *American Journal of Sociology*, XLII, No. 2 (September, 1936), 234-37.

The heat in the argument over the word is another of the interesting by-products of race relations. Some students insist that the term should not be applied to the bi-racial system of this country, but kept as the proper name for the categories of India. If we grant this we will simply have to find some other term to stand for the kind of social category into which one is assigned by birth and from which he cannot escape by any actions of his own; and to distinguish such social categories from classes or ranked groups, from which it is possible, though sometimes difficult, to rise.

5. Warner, *Ibid.*, p. 235.

by a line, horizontal in slavery days but now tilted, for some
Negroes are of higher class than some whites. In a similar
diagram, Park shows the caste line as swung to the vertical,
with the two races looking across at one another on a level.[6]
Things have not gone so far as that—not yet. Warner's chart
shows more accurately the present position of the classes in
Negro society with relation to the classes in white society. A
considerable and ever increasing number of Negroes stand,
by all standards except that of the social definition of race
itself, above many white people. But caste remains, for in
certain matters, particularly in courtship and marriage, the
race-caste criterion of status prevails over all others; yet it is
perhaps ignored in more circumstances than ever before.

And here we come to a paradox. Negroes apparently rise
to the middle-class level of education, work, and way of living relatively more often in North America, where there is
a strict race-caste line, than do American Indian and Negro
people in Latin America, where there is scarcely any race
line at all. James Bryce [7] noted that color is no barrier to
marriage in Latin America, if only the individual is of the
right social accomplishments and wealth, but that in most of
the Latin countries the masses of the people (Indian, mestizo,
Negro and mulatto) are so marked off from the whiter middle classes by poverty that few of them rise. North America
combines one of the most open class systems of the world with
a strict race line; South America combines absence of race
line with tight kin-classes, and relatively small opportunity
for the dark-skinned masses to rise. North America oppresses
the Negro, but founds dozens of schools and colleges which
help him to climb. In spite of segregation of Negroes in inferior schools, in spite of discrimination in employment, great
numbers have risen to middle-class positions.

Every civilization has its own ladders by which people may
climb from miserable to better positions, and its own special
obstacles. Race and ethnic lines may appear either among

---

6. Park, *ibid.*, p. 243.
7. *South America: Observations and Impressions* (New York: Macmillan,
1912), p. 474.

the assets or the liabilities of people in a social system. But they are only one among may factors which determine the general social metabolism. For, as Schumpeter insists, [8] the rise and fall of individuals and families from class to class, and the rise and fall of classes themselves within a class system, go on whether or not there be ethnic differences. In our world the signs of status are so frequently ethnic, however, that the struggle of the individual to rise and of groups to improve their position by political means, are often, in fact, ethnic struggles.

Most of our discussion of status has grown out of cases in which one group gains rather complete dominance over another. This is not the typical situation of a national or ethnic minority, such as the French in Canada, the Flemish in contact with Walloons in Belgium, and the Poles in their older contact with Germans or Russians. In all of these cases the "minority" people showed a fairly complete range of classes. The politically dominant invading people were aware of this and the upper classes of the two groups recognized each other as such. No German in Poland thought that a landed Polish aristocrat who spoke *salon* French was a peasant. Very few English Canadians are so ethnocentric as to assume that a French-Canadian aristocrat or scholar is an uncultured fellow.

In all of these cases the class system of the minority was based on a less industrial economy than that of the invading group. The French-English frontier in Canada may be taken as a fair example. The French had settled down in Canada by the time of the English conquest. There were among them peasants, lumberjacks, artisans, small-town business and professional men, merchants, small manufacturers, scholars, aristocrats. Social classes were well developed, and there were some people of aristocratic temper and pretension. The military conquest did not change all of this to any extent; for,

---

8. Joseph Schumpeter, *Imperialism and Social Classes* (New York: Augustus M. Keeley, Inc., 1951), see "Social Classes in an Ethnically Homogeneous Environment."

as Mannheim says, [9] a mere military conquest generally does not deeply affect a social structure. The real shock came from the continued impact of the aggressively commercial English civilization, and eventually of an industrial civilization. The Englishmen who came to Quebec were not landed gentry, but merchants on the make.

Now, when industry comes to a Quebec town, the local French middle and upper classes have little to offer it except that political liaison which will make the industry comfortable by keeping taxes down. Some of the young English (Canadian or American) men brought to town by an industry may add to the charm of life and to their own social position by marrying daughters of outstanding French families. English people who want to grace their money with class have been doing this in Quebec for a century and a half. But few of the young French men of the middle class have the training to step into middle positions in industry. The new industrial labor force is recruited from the working classes of the local French people and from the farms, which produce more children than the land can accommodate. The French Canadians who rise within industry will probably *not* be the sons of the French middle class of the pre-industrial era, for these young men are trained for law, medicine, and similar professions, for those things that were valued in the old culture, not for the work of modern industry. The advantages they have in the older society carry but little weight in the new industrial order.

In this, and in the many similar cases, an alien ethnic group brings a new industrial order to a people whose class distinctions have grown up about another order, based on land, small businesses and industries, and the professions. The lower classes of the local people find the possibilities of making a living expanded, and they can, to some small extent, rise in the new order. The middle and upper classes, on the contrary, find their chances withering away. More than

---

9. Karl Mannheim, "Ueber das Wesen und die Bedeutung des wirtschaftlichen Erfolgsstrebens," *Archiv für Sozialwissenschaft und Sozialpolitik*, LXIII, No. 3 (June, 1930), 449-512.

that, the people who used to pay them deference now move in a new order of things, with alien employers—who control their livings and their chances to climb up in the world. Class deference may, in due time, be paid not to the traditional betters, but to the new economic betters, the aliens.

Thus is created, not a status fault but a status strain. While neither group is rated above the other in social rank, the classes with most advantages in the older order suffer a status wound. The old ways of mobility, to which family ambitions and the educational system are geared, lose their effectiveness. The generation of young men who discover this, to their sorrow, may become leaders of an "out with the aliens" movement. Their anger is that of a man who, just after he has staked all, finds that he was playing by the wrong rules. The bottom class of the minority group suffers no immediate status loss. But in the new order there is a *de facto* distinction of status between native "minority" and alien. For the aliens who bring the new industrial order will be concentrated in number greater than chance in the middle and upper ranks of industry, while the native minority will be at the bottom.

It thus comes about that the native minority has, in fact, a weighting in the lower classes while the new group has a weighting in the middle classes. In some Quebec towns there are no lower-class English people at all, for all English inhabitants were brought to fill technical and managerial positions in industry. Such a statistical or *de facto* difference of the distribution of two peoples among the ranks may in time come to be supported by sentiments. There are English people who have in their minds a stereotype of the French-Canadian as a man of lower class and little education.

Something like this happens whenever industry goes into a region where a less industrialized people of western civilization have an established class system. The sequence of events and the sentiments aroused are probably of much the same kind whether the ethnic difference is great or small.

Chapter Eight

Nations, States and Gods

Lurking in many of the ethnic and racial problems of our time has been the concept of the nation-state. According to it the ideal sovereign political unit, or state, is one whose territorial boundaries are clear-cut lines, so thin that, when a gate is opened, a single stride will take one right out of his own country into the next. Within the boundaries all the people are of one racial stock, one language, one tradition and, in the purest case, of one religion. These people compose the nation; state (government) and nation (a people) coincide at all points. Sometimes the people are considered to be of a common ancestry; or even to be descended from certain heroic individuals. Such ancestry is, of course, a social myth, a powerful collective symbol which holds people together.

A purely territorial state claims sovereignty over all within its boundaries, including the ethnic strangers within its gates. A purely national state would claim sovereignty over its members no matter where they go. It would disregard territory. The nation-state suffers from continual strain because it combines these two contradictory principles. At least they are contradictory in a world in which people move around.

Countries which have received immigrants have modified their concept of nation by allowing and encouraging people to be naturalized, thus sharing in the common spiritual ancestry. The Pilgrims and the signers of the Declaration of Independence become thereby forefathers of the children of Sicilian immigrants. Countries of emigration, on the other hand, have been rather inclined to insist that a person cannot resign from his nation.

A deeper stress has come from the paradoxical combination of the idea of nation-state with that of the expanding state. The healthy nation-state is not a tight little island, embattled against all invaders; it expands in population, prosperity, and political power. It has a world mission. The very peoples who did most to develop the concept of the nation-state have been also the most active agents of modern empire—prior to the expansion of the Soviet empire.

In spite of the power of the nation-state idea there is no pure case in reality. Holland and Denmark are close to it, but their boundaries are not as thin and clear as the ideal. The villages on their peripheries are generally ethnically homogeneous, but are not so arranged that all those of one language and culture fall neatly on either side of the boundary. This is generally true of rural ethnic boundaries in Europe. Matters are further complicated by the tendency throughout history for people of one ethnic kind to found trading towns and cities in territory where rural villagers are of another kind. Cities are often strange ethnically as well as in mode of life.

Reality departs from the ideal of the nation-state by reason of the simple fact that ethnic boundaries are not usually clear, but also because of the political processes by which states and their boundaries are made; the balance of political and military power does not always come to rest at ethnic boundaries. Some states combine two or more ethnic groups into one political people; thus the Flemings and the French-speaking Walloons compose the Belgian people, and thus people of three languages are Swiss. The United Kingdom includes the Welsh and Scottish as well as the English. There are people of Germanic dialect in France. There are Basques in France and Spain; Frisians in the Netherlands and Germany. In some such cases a formerly important language is reduced to being a dialect or a vehicle of folklore, regarded as quaint by those of the bigger world. Folk culture may shrivel as dialects give way to a more literate school-nourished national language. (The parochial dialect, to use Bagehot's phrase, has not yet become the sole national language.) The people may, in such a case, fully accept membership in the nation-state in which they live; but sometimes they do not, and become instead a defensive, self-conscious national minority.

In America, political boundaries were generally set before the adjacent country was fully settled. That simplified matters to some extent, but we have had boundary problems even in North America. Canada still thinks she was done on the Maine and Alaska boundaries; she is not quite sure which of her dearest friends did it—perfidious mother Albion or that sharp Yankee trader, Uncle Sam. The boundary between the French Canadians and Yankees never was clear and never did correspond to the political boundary. Vermont Yankees settled over the border in the Eastern townships of Quebec at an early date and just kept on celebrating the Fourth of July. French Canadians filtered down into rural New England even before Yankees turned to building cotton mills and sought a large part of their labor force in Quebec. But the political boundary between Canada and the United States appears settled, although it is not and never has been an ethnic or linguistic one.

Our boundary disputes to the south and west we settled to our great satisfaction by expanding so as to take in French and Spanish-speaking peoples who were thus made into minorities.

In South America the boundary disputes have been related not so much to ethnic matters as simply to political power and control of resources. Many miles of boundaries still lie practically unexplored in forests and mountains, and are still controversial. But the countries of South America, like those of North America, are of great and recent ethnic mixture.

Some, especially Brazil, are still actively receiving immigrants from Europe and Africa, and have large colonies of people who speak other than the official language. The nation-state ideal is, in the Americas, a projection into the future, although there are people in our country who like to think that some time in our past we were closer to it than now.

Religion often enters into questions of ethnic and national identity. The role of religion in the quarrel between England and Ireland is expressed in the formerly-current saying: "If England went Catholic today, Ireland would be Protestant tomorrow." Christianity is a religion of universal, not ethnic, symbols: one of its largest divisions is called Catholic, which means universal. The Hitlerites, in fact, reproached Christianity for being universal and thus departing from "true" racial and ethnic doctrine. Yet the particular forms of Christianity have tended to be ethnic, and even racial.

The Scandinavian countries probably approach the ideal of the religiously homogeneous nation-state more closely than have any others; at least, there have been times when they approached it. The Protestant Reformation in its northern European form of the separation of national churches from Rome was most complete there. It was some time before pietistic and evangelical sects made inroads on the national churches. These countries still have only a handful of Catholics and Jews.

In Germany, as in England, a religious reformation was one part of the rise of nationalism. Each German principality and kingdom for long had its state religion, Protestant or Catholic. Later mixing changed the distribution. Protestantism was the religion of Prussia, and Prussians wondered whether the Rheinlanders and other Catholics could be true Germans. To a certain kind of North German patriot they are still suspect. The expression *die preussische Sendung*—the Prussian mission—stood for a kind of religious—definitely Lutheran—economic and political calling of the Prussians.

Of the modern western religions the Jewish faith is the only one which is frankly ethnic. The very fact that Jews are proud of *not* proselytizing symbolizes their sentiment that the true Jew is the born Jew. The Christian churches and sects preserve the fiction that no one is quite born a Christian. They have to baptize him or perform some gesture to make him a little bit of a Christian, and provide a rather modified little hell for him to go to, a limbo, if he does not get baptized at all. The Christians are ambivalent on the question whether one is born into Christianity or not, but one is quite frankly born into the Jewish group.

In recent times the national element in Jewry has been revived and the territory which was for many many generations and centuries only a symbol and a shrine now has a political aim and a political reality. This is one of the paradoxes of our time, and a good illustration of the dialectic between the religious and the ethnic or national idea, for in Israel, the Jewish homeland, we see the contrast between the notion of a Mecca in the sense of a general symbol, as against a sacred, but *political,* territory of a people. Now all the great religions have had their Meccas, places of pilgrimages, their historic holy places. The Far East is full of them, Lhasa being perhaps the greatest; Rome is the great shrine for a large proportion of the Christians; and Jerusalem is a Holy Place for Jewry and for Christendom and Islam as well. But the idea of the Mecca, the holy place, sometimes gets mixed up with ethnic conceptions of the Holy Soil, enriched by the blood of the ancestors, the ancient seat of a people. Ancestors and saints, the ancestors of a people and the saints of a religion, are a little hard to tell apart in any case. George slaying the dragon on behalf of the English is also St. George. The confusion of ancestral folk-heroes with Christian saints is notorious, for both, the ancestor and the saint, are symbols of an historical social entity to which people belong. Likewise, the Mecca and the sacred soil of the forefathers where a people lives or has a sacred right to live, also are symbols of something to which they belong and it is not always clear, again, which is which.

In the case of the modern Jews, the two ideas of the symbolic scene of the ancient altars and of a political territory which of right belongs to them, have blended into one of the fiercest movements of modern times. It is so widespread a movement that it is not exaggerating to say that probably every Jewish Sabbath-school leaflet in every synagogue or temple throughout this country links religion with politics in Israel in an inextricable mixture, making of them one and the same thing. What was a philanthropy of the Jews of western Europe on behalf of the Jews of eastern Europe, a social agency to provide a place of refuge at a convenient distance from one's own front door, has, thanks to Hitlerism, become the center of one of the most powerful political movements of our time.

Ironically, when the Jewish people of the western world, and of Russia when Communism came to power, had got to the point of their strongest identification in history with the countries in which they lived—just then, of all times, the Nazis accused them of being traitors. Of course, the reasons for the Nazis making those accusations at that time had not much to do with the historic situation of the Jews, and especially not of the German Jews who were so assimilated as to be almost unaware of their Jewishness. But it had a great deal to do with the historic situation of Germany at that moment. Just at that point in Jewish history the Nazis accused them of having stabbed Germany in the back (thus causing Germany to lose the First World War), of having caused the decline of the folk virtues in favor of the urban vices, of having divided loyalties (or rather, no loyalties except to one another), and of cherishing world-wide political designs. The Nazis then proceeded, presumably because of these alleged sins, to a great mass persecution carried out with unbelievable torture and cruelty, a massacre whose horror of method and whose magnitude cannot be exaggerated. It was by this program that the Nazis made their own accusation come true in part, for the Jews of the western world, in their extremity and fear, felt driven to form political pressure groups in every country in which they lived. So at present there is probably more division of political loyalty among Jews than ever before in modern times, because the notion of political loyalty to Palestine, dead for centuries and centuries, now lives again among them.

This whole series of events and reactions is related to modern national-state politics, and to the notion of the nation-state, and, at the same time, to the history of capitalism and the history of empire. This is an intriguing mixture which, let us hope, some one will undertake to sort out in a thorough and masterly way.

Now the Christian religion is equally interesting in its relation to racial, ethnic and national phenomena. The movement started with, if you allow the word, a de-ethnicizing. The New Testament tells of it in those terms. Many of the stories have to do with the breaking away from ethnic symbols, or of their interpretation in some new broader way. Peter has, you will remember, a nightmare in which there is let down before him "unclean" (not kosher) food. Shall he eat it or not? In his dream he decides to eat it because there is another non-ethnic, non-kosher, standard of cleanliness, one more spiritual and less material, which he now takes for his own. That is a story of being detribalized. The story of the conversion of St. Paul is another. His Epistles contain arguments back and forth concerning Greek standards, Jewish standards, and the relation of the ethnic rule to the more universal, non-ethnic, in the religion of the future. He was addressing confused people who were trying to find a way for themselves, and who found it in a non-ethnic religion.

In due time Christianity, as it spread, got mixed up with the ethnic religions of all the countries around the Mediterranean. A variety of ethnic branches and versions grew up, along with sectarian varieties. Then these were in some measure drawn together by Rome, which dominated the church. This was followed by the break-up into the two great clusters, Roman in the west, Byzantine in the east, corresponding to the two great centers of culture and civilization and the two seats of imperial domination. Thus, the first dialectic was as between ethnic Jewish and the non-ethnic or supra-ethnic, followed by division into regional and sectarian branches, and the drawing of these together into a new imperial church, so that Roman culture was Christian catholic culture. Christianity became more ethnic again in the Reformation, when the various national forms of Protestantism grew up.

As, through the ages, the church spread, there were doctrinal movements whose leaders became either saints or heretics, according to the way the wind blew—for every saint must be almost a heretic. Every nation and almost every region of Europe produced its favorite hero-saint, and the movements whereby they were made expressed the peculiarities and aspirations of the local ethnic elements. The French Joan of Arc was, in fact, burned at the stake and later canonized as part of a French movement in Catholicism. She was the perfect combination of national heroine and saint, whose very sanctity lay in her heroic role in a holy national movement. There is a constant play, in Christianity, between universal symbols, embracing all humanity, and local ethnic realities, ethnic discontents, and the growth of new regional feelings and identities. No doubt the same dialectic between universal human symbols and local, ethnic, kin, race, and national symbols can be found in the East.

In the United States almost every church is significantly ethnic in its history, and retains some measure of ethnic character. Thus our central group of Protestant churches—Presbyterian, Congregational, Episcopalian, Unitarian, Methodist, Baptist—are all of them deposits of movements which took place in England. At some crucial point in the history of the movement the people migrated out here, so the history of the movement is one of class and other social changes in England, followed by migration and continuation of the movement in America. Professor William W. Sweet, who has done a great deal of research on religion on the American frontier,[1] likes to point out that the Methodists and Baptists came through the woods, down the rivers on flat boats; the

---

1. In a series of volumes entitled *Religion on the American Frontier, 1783–1850.*

Presbyterians waited for the turnpikes, and the Episcopalians didn't come until they could get Pullman reservations.

These churches, together with the more aloof churches of the German, Dutch and Scandinavian immigrants, form the main body of American Protestantism. Members and even ministers move from one to another, seeking whatever combination of convenience, social compatibility and style of religious expression best suits them. The churches, like their individual members, show a strong tendency to move toward the middle class. Their progress leaves a trail of stricter Bible sects each of which claims to preserve or restore the original spirit of the movement. Methodist Protestants and Primitive Methodists split off from the Methodist Episcopal church more than a century ago. Nazarenes and various so-called Churches of God took their turns later in protesting departure from strict Biblical injunction. They, too, have moved toward respectability and middle-class decorum in religious expression. Still newer store-front and Bible-hall sects are taking their place, finding followers among the poorer of rural migrants to the city who find the urban churches of their traditional denominations too liberal in theology and too restrained in expression. It remains to be seen whether they will send their latest converts, like those of earlier sects, on the disciplined road to social mobility—and, by the same token, back to the very churches they left.

The ethnic history and struggles of Catholicism in America are less known than those of Protestantism. Catholic historians use Lord Baltimore of Maryland, the French exploring missionaries and the French Catholics of Louisiana to prove that Catholics, too, had their part in founding the country. But the main body of American Catholics consists of more recent immigrants and their descendants. The American Catholic Church has taken its present character mainly from the struggles of these more recent immigrants with America and with one another.

The first of the European Catholics to become established in the United States in number were the Irish. They became dominant in the northeastern cities and there they laid down the pattern of *territorial* parishes. Now the Catholic Church believes in the basic territorial parish as the final unit of church administration. One is supposed to be baptized, married, and buried in his own parish, that is, the parish within which his family resides. But when the German, Austrian, Italian, Polish, Lithuanian, and other Catholics arrived from Europe and the French from Quebec, they succeeded in having their own parishes set up, with their own clergy and parochial schools. These were called *national*. Thus in sections of Chicago, an Irish, a German, a Lithuanian, and two Polish Catholic churches (for the faithful from two provinces back in Poland), may stand within a few blocks of each other. Such national parishes may be superimposed upon the original territorial parishes. (In the province of Quebec the position of the Irish is reversed: the basic territorial parishes, lying contiguous to each other like the wards in a city or townships in the country, are French, while the "national" parishes are Irish. The Irish don't like it.)

Now many of the local ethnic parishes were in the jurisdiction of dioceses whose bishops were Irish. Certain of the German, Austrian and other Catholics considered the Irish as unintellectual and rather good-will-ish after the manner of American Protestants, and sought to get rid of the Irish leadership in church administration. They demanded *national dioceses*. This would mean a German church, an Italian church, and so on, nation-wide and each under its own bishop. What was actually revolt against the Irish took the form of a movement to define the American church as a mission church, to be organized according to a principle often used in mission regions whereby certain bishops control certain ethnic groups rather than all the souls in a territory. But in the end the *territorial diocese* was firmly, once and for all, established in the American church, and in many dioceses, the Irish, already strongly entrenched, continue to have the upper hand.

Some of the Catholic orders in this country are strongly identified with one ethnic group or another. The Society of the Divine Word (S.V.D.) is definitely German in its recruiting and its leadership. It runs missions for Negroes, Mexicans and other underprivileged ethnic groups, and is known among other Catholics as the "Send Vun Dollar" order since it solicits money in small sums from any and all. The Franciscans also seem to be somewhat German. Other orders are dominated by Catholics of other origins. Each order tries to find for itself a set of functions in this country as it had in Europe. Some have taken over the function of educating the growing numbers of American Catholic mobile upper-middle-class girls in exclusive convents. As the place of Catholics in American society becomes more varied and solid, the orders find new functions.

The ethnic struggle goes on between parishes as well. Nearly every parish has an ethnic history and an historic ethnic identification. But, just as the ethnic groups tend to get different class positions according as they are older or younger in America, so the corresponding parishes in a city tend to find their position in a prestige ranking. It is as a rule in most parts of the country a parish of Irish origin that becomes the "classy" one. In the course of time certain conflicts arise between the parishes of a city. They reflect to some extent the ethnic composition of the parishes. When the "classy" parish notes that many of its children are going to high school, it will want to establish a Catholic high school. It usually finds the project too big and must enlist cooperation from other parishes. There is at present a great increase of Catholic high schools in this country, each as a rule supported by several parishes. Establishing a high school creates the occasion for the conflict between the parishes to come to a head and to be composed. It gives the despised ethnic parishes some bargaining power to improve their position in relation to the dominant American (Irish) parish of the town.

The ethnic conflict may turn up within the individual parish. The Catholic parish in this country, like its Protestant counterpart, is an enterprise. It is usually built up by one man, an energetic priest who inspires a few zealous families. (This idea would be impossible to understand in Europe, where every parish is an historical entity, usually centuries old, and tax-supported.) Leadership in a successful American parish-building enterprise is a way of mobility to the Catholic clergy, just as it is to the man who wants to be a Methodist bishop: he builds a big church, and leaves a handsome debt behind for some other fellow to clean up after he himself has moved up to the higher place. Moreover, to a number of Irish families, the parish is the symbol of middle-class status, evidence that they have risen enough in the world to own property and to build a large church with a large mortgage in a desirable residential district, and for the women to form altar guilds to keep flowers on the altar and to set up the auxiliary organizations that one finds in Protestant middle-class churches in America. Thus each parish which has something approaching middle-class standing represents a great achievement for some group of people.

Now, if it comes to pass that there is an ethnic or racial invasion in the neighborhood where priests and people have built up this collective and symbolic enterprise, they are deeply disturbed. This brings about an inconsistency in the church: while the Franciscans and the S.V.D. are establishing missions, parishes, schools and social centers for Negroes, certain independent Catholic parishes may vigorously oppose ethnic and racial invasion of their neighborhoods. There are parishes in which the parishioners frankly say they don't worry about the invasion of Negroes, because "Father will look after that." The good Father is doing what one finds in so many human organizations: he is acting on the side of what he would call "reality,"—although he would probably rise and smite you if you were to suggest that he is rather less than completely Christian on the point of race relations. If Protestants—and Jews—notice this in the Catholic church, it is because ethnocentrism is in part a sharp eye for contradictions in *other* groups and cultures!

In the phase which American Catholicism is now entering we may see the emerging of a general Catholic culture, distinctly American. This no doubt involves a number of processes, such as the achievement of a sure middle-class position by a large number of American Catholics. The Catholic population has been weighted in the lower class, so that many aspects of the American Protestant's definition of Catholicism or of Catholic people have been simply a part of his definition of lower-class behavior: he confuses class with religion. Raffles and street carnivals and bingo games are thought to be Catholic here. In Quebec, an upper-middle-class parish is outraged by these things—no, not outraged, for they think such activities are proper for a working-class parish. In America, Catholics sense that many Protestants think Catholics are of low class. James Farrell's books are, in effect, a bitter account of Irish Catholic efforts to rise economically and socially in a country where the models of success are Protestant.

As Catholics get into the middle class, there will be, indeed there already is, a merging of the ethnic elements. In the merging we would predict that Irish patterns will predominate over German. The Knights of Columbus, for instance, never took hold in German-American Catholicism. It is only as the Irish model is followed that one finds them. The Polish Catholics, as they become assimilated, follow the Irish and form chapters of the Knights of Columbus with baseball teams. Someone should study the growth of the Irish-American pattern, and the following of it as a model by other ethnic groups of Catholics.

The peculiarity of the position of the Catholic church in this country, a thing which distinguishes it from the Catholicism of western Europe, is that the upper-middle-class models of behavior have here always been Protestant. That is a great danger to the church, for it means that mobility is movement toward Protestantism. That is why the Church has had to permit the Knights of Columbus, although it is a kind of Catholic Free Masonry, something the bishops have not liked in modern times. It grew up in New Haven among Catholic railway men, railroad work having been one of the important ways to moderate social and economic mobility for the Irish in America. As they got into the jobs of locomotive engineer and conductor, they got middle-class ideas.

After considerable conflict the organization was permitted. Then this great fraternal order apparently followed the trend of Free Masonry itself, which after an early period when its strength was in the upper-middle class, is definitely falling toward the lower-middle class. The upper-middle-class Protestant men nowadays join the Masons only as evidence that they belong on the right side and can be counted on in a pinch, and are good fellows. In like manner, American Catholics who are getting higher in the class scale are said to lose interest in the Knights of Columbus. If this is so, two trends are involved: ethnic assimilation and the growing influence of the existing Protestant class symbols.

The American Catholics, one suspects, combine a certain desire to be like other people with a very human tendency to be aggressive against them. An example is the tie of Catholic organizations and colleges in America with athletics, a connection which is incomprehensible to Catholics from any other part of the world. Thousands of Catholic boys in the poorer parts of Chicago know only two things about Notre Dame University: that it is Catholic and that its football team can beat the boys of the essentially Protestant Ivy League colleges at their own game.

The auxiliary organizations in American Catholicism appear to vary from one ethnic group to another. Their original purpose may have been to preserve the ethnic culture, or to protect people from the hazards of life in America, but they all seem to be approaching a common type. In many respects—in composition, basis of membership, causes and programs—the new type appears to be like the corresponding institutions of middle-class Protestant churches. The adaptation of the Catholic church to American society and institutions may turn out to have been the most important series of events in Catholic history in the twentieth century. It will be no less important for American society and institutions.

Chapter Nine

What's in a Name?

"Oh, be some other name!
What's in a name? That which we call a rose
By any other name would smell as sweet:
So Romeo would, were he not Romeo called,
Retain that dear perfection which he owes,
Without that title. Romeo, doff thy name;
And for that name, which is no part of thee,
Take all myself."

Romeo and Juliet, Act II, Sc. 2

There is generally a great deal in a name, as Juliet plainly knew. Often it is more than a pointer; it points with pride, or with the finger of scorn. It may contain a caricature which, by emphasizing some one trait, distorts as well as designates. This is notoriously so when groups of people are naming one another.

In science, the name of a chemical element, a ray, a law, is supposed merely to denote. Therefore the name itself is of no particular significance: a letter will do. A Greek letter is best of all; since nowadays Greek really is Greek to most people the letter will have no other meaning in their minds than the one which the scientist arbitrarily assigns to it. And yet even scientists are not always indifferent to names. Since it has become the custom to name a thing after its discoverer, the name alleges a historical fact on which scientists may be somewhat less agreed than on the facts of science itself—and there is no experiment or ordeal by which the event may be repeated and the allegation of fact tested. Because pride in priority of discovery is one of the mainsprings of scientific effort and a source of conflict among scientists, such names may provoke very strong feeling. Sometimes, too, the scientist finds that a name which, perhaps, he gave in all innocence has unfortunate popular connotations: nicotinic acid, a vitamin, was recently renamed niacin, at the insistence, it seems, of the anti-cigaret ladies—who are also great supporters of nutrition programs. But for the most part scientific names are not the objects of feeling but are purely pointers.

In the social sciences pride of discovery is the least of the problems of naming things. Professor Frank Knight has pointed to a more serious difficulty; namely, that our concepts tend to become epithets. He has left out half the process, for at least in sociology many concepts were epithets before we took them up. In fact, a considerable part of sociology consists of cleaning up the language in which common people talk of social and moral problems. We make great effort to make bad things better by change of name, and we try, too, to make things disappear by giving them bad names. This used to be called exorcism.

Since the subject matter of sociology, at any rate, and perhaps of all social science that is in fact social, is precisely the matter about which people have convictions, prejudices, hates, the things about which they praise or blame one another, it would be rather too much to expect our concepts to be as free of popular feeling and distortion as are most names in chemistry or physics. We could achieve merely denotative names in social science, but it would be at the price of having no communication between social scientists and the lay public.

Our work, as a matter of fact, requires two kinds of communication. One is that by which we get our data. We reach down among the people (most of us came from there, too) and dip up our findings. They come to us in the rich vocabulary of popular speech. Even a census family card is a translation from the vernacular in which names are not merely pointers, but are weighted with sentiments.

This kind of communication, by which we learn about people from people, has its own particular hazards. Since we may be trying to make the world better by getting rid of prejudices, it is hard for us to listen quietly when people make nasty prejudiced remarks. It gives the young social scientist nightmares to hear people give vent to their biases, but he must learn to face it. The priest, too, has to learn to listen to confessions and in time he may take a somewhat humorous and detached view of them so that he finds himself occasionally reminding people that they are there to confess and not to boast! Let us hope that we will never grow so sanctimonious that we cannot listen to the mean things people say. They are our data. We must never close off the channels to them.

The other kind of communication is that by which we report our findings, our analyses and our interpretations to various professional and lay publics. Some social scientists protect themselves by taking refuge in an invented lingo. But that does not always succeed, for some publics simply take over the new words. It is an open question whether that is a good thing either for the public or for social science. A more important question is whether the invented lingo was good in the first place.

If, however, the social scientists' communication is to be effective, it requires some use of popular language. At once that introduces the possibility that the people we study will also be our readers. The anthropologists have an easier time. There is, it is true, some searching of heart among them as to the effectiveness of the first kind of communication, that by which they collect their data. Since they gather their material often from one or two informants and frequently in a language other than that of the culture being studied, they sometimes must ask themselves if they are getting the real stuff. But the second kind of communication, the reporting of data, presents almost no problem to them. Not because of the nature of their science but because their traditional subject matter has been primitive, preliterate, or exotic peoples, aliens to their culture (or, to put it the other way around, to whose culture the anthropologists are alien), they run little risk that the people they write about will ever read their reports. When all the peoples of the earth can read, the anthropologists' concepts will lose their immunity from popular connotations and will be subject to the same risks as the sociologists'.

While we must be ready for the possibility that our subjects will be our readers, we should also recognize that people will not always read what we write, though enough may do so to make trouble. When the people of "Middletown" put a copy of Robert and Helen Lynd's book about them in the cornerstone of a public building, the local Democratic newspaper (whose sharpness of tongue may be accounted for by the fact that there are not many Democrats in the town), is said to have remarked that if people had read the book they never would have put it there for posterity to see. As a matter of fact sociologists are not sure whether they *want* people to read what they have said. Just what audience they do want is not clear.

It is hard to say whether sociologists—including graduate students getting their first lessons in substituting big words for knowledge—or the public, do most of the corrupting of sociological terms. We live in an age, as Gustav Ichheiser has observed, in which words are exceptionally likely to be considered good or bad, in which we try to manipulate things by changing names a great deal. It is an age in which people will stoutly deny doing anything which has come to have a bad name, at least they will deny it by that name. The corollary is that they will stay away from something that has been given too nice a name.

To illustrate: In studying race relations in industry we discovered that there is no such thing—in Chicago, at any rate—as an industry which indulges in racial discrimination. Discrimination is something which no decent, self-respecting American does—by that name, anyway. The industries did not discriminate, but their managers and personnel men acted on "knowledge" of "the facts." They "knew" that some people are better at the kind of work they wanted done in their factories. (Since this is a world in which we do everything because we "know," because we have the engineering mentality of deciding on the basis of facts and science, we can do nothing without believing that we "know." We must then stretch our "knowledge" so that we can act.) They "knew" all about the working capacities even of kinds of people whom they had never hired at all. But then we discovered that no industry can really tell how much women can produce as compared with men, or Negroes as compared with whites; reliable information on the point scarcely exists. Once we were asked into a plant which made a point of integrating Negroes into its working force, and which was quite sure its records would show that Negroes produced as much as whites. But we found that the Negroes were working on the oldest, slowest machines in the place, while the white workers, who had been there longer and who were closely connected by kin and friendship, had all the nice new machines. We pointed out that with conditions so unequal there was no way of telling whether Negroes produced more or less than white workers. The management was distinctly disappointed.

Another rationalization is that one does not discriminate, but simply does not want to disturb the harmony of his organization by introducing some strange breed of people whom his present employees wouldn't like. A hotel manager says he doesn't discriminate against Negro guests, but that his policy is made by his customers; he does what they want and doesn't do what they wouldn't like. This raises the fundamental question concerning "other-directed" business and professional men—to use Mr. Riesman's term—namely, when the customer is always right, which customer is it who is right? And how do you find out which one is right and what he thinks?

Since discrimination is bad, people don't admit doing it. We ought to have anticipated this human propensity to sidestep a name, for among the best known processes of philology are the repeated attempts, throughout history, to find some nicer and more acceptable words for parts and processes of the human body. Every religious movement of a puritanical sort casts out old names and compels people to invent new circumlocutions. The doctors use Latin or scientific terms,

Latin being for historic reasons more scientific among us than Anglo-Saxon.

In spite of this age-long substitution of new names each time the old ones got bad, the parts and the processes of the body continue with us. So does discrimination—under whatever name or phrase is currently acceptable.

Now for an instance of running away from a nice name: I was lately asked to go down to a university in the southern border counties of a northern state, to take part in a panel discussion of race and ethnic relations. The advance publicity, however, said nothing of race relations, but talked of "human relations." When I got there the news was gently broken to me that only a dozen or so of the two hundred school teachers invited were coming to the Conference on Human Relations, though they could have had the day off with pay! It came out that everyone knew that "human relations" means race relations. Either the school teachers were not going to be preached at about race relations, or they thought it not wise, in that region, to take a day off to attend a conference on race relations.

Of course, the organizers of this conference were merely following the trend. For nearly all the committees, commissions, and other public bodies set up to deal with race relations are now called by the supposedly broader, and more neutral and disarming, name of "human relations," or "intergroup relations." Naturally, people are perfectly well aware of the change and of the hidden meanings of "human relations." It is like the experience of a pediatrician whose nurse gave a lollypop to each child brought to the office. This worked well with most children, but one used to scream at the very sight of a lollypop. One wonders, by the way, why no one has thought of making "human" into a bad word. What we would do then it is hard to imagine.

This brings up the whole matter of the distortion of concepts in our culture in general, and in social science in particular. "Tolerance" is an example. In our society a thing which we tolerate is something which we must not discuss, or at least not criticize. It is something whose presence we must allow without raising questions. It is intolerant if we say to a Catholic friend, "I still think it is all wrong to withhold the wine from communicants." The tolerant thing is to say that we differ in our belief and behavior. As things are now, a controversial question has come to mean a question about which you must have no controversy.

A third example is more crucially pertinent to race relations: the terminology of prejudice and discrimination. Two serious and capable students of race relations, Arnold and Caroline Rose, on the first page of their book *America Divided*,[1] give this definition: "The mere fact of being generally hated because of religious, racial, or nationality background is what defines a minority group." They go on to explain why they avoid the word "prejudice" in the definition: "There is nothing intrinsically wrong with the term 'prejudice' and we would use it but for the fact that it has gradually assumed an aura of respectability, or at least of ceremonial, in the average man's mind, which it is not intended to have by the experts." In other words, they must have a word that is worse than "prejudice," and they turn to the word "hate." What will they do when "hate" wears out? If we follow this course we cast off first one word, then another, as words get nicer, and replace them with worse words—thus modifying the meaning of a great many words in our language and giving our science a new vocabulary every year or so.

Then there is the word "discrimination." The authors posit that a minority problem exists if people are hated and discriminated against, meaning by the word "harmful things . . . done to people solely because of their race, religion or nationality." Discrimination is thus the harmful action inspired by our hatred. Now, according to this new definition of minority, the French Canadians, for example, are either generally hated or they are not a minority. This means we will simply have to find other terms in which to speak of such peoples as the French Canadians, the Flemings, and

---

1. New York: Alfred A. Knopf, 1948, pp. 3-5.

others, historically called minorities, who, by war or change of political boundary, have been thrown into countries dominated by languages and cultures other than theirs. For if the word "minority" is used it means we are declaring we hate these people. (Instead of saying "I hate you," from now on we need only say, "You minority bird, you!")

Hate is, one need hardly say, one of the greatest of human —and hence of sociological—problems; but if we define minority, prejudice, and discrimination, concepts that are basic to the discussion and analysis of interracial and interethnic processes, in epithetical terms, the student will associate them with their popular connotations and in many cases there will be no minority, by definition!

Incidentally, the new definitions pose a new problem which the authors leave unsettled: who is the referee to decide which group hates the other the more and thereby escapes being the minority?

There is a mild minor case of change of meaning in the word "ethnic." All human beings used to belong to ethnic groups—all, that is, but the marginal men, who are caught between two groups. But now we are beginning to speak of some people as ethnic and others as not. If, in any community, n is the number of groups by the old definition, then n $minus$ 1 is the number of groups by the new definition. There is one which is *not* ethnic; that is, the charter-member ethnic group of the community; and there are the people who *are* ethnic, namely, all those who differ from it and, by implication, have something less than full standing in the local society. Now we will have to find a new term which will include the charter-members, as well as the others, a term which will have the same meaning if used in some other society as when used to refer to American conditions. We keep doing these little tricks with words apparently because, in social science, we think we have discovered something when we have invented a name.

The wearing out and distorting of concepts in our field often registers a change in point of view or intention. A long

time ago we began calling child criminals "juvenile delin-
quents." The new name expressed a change in attitude which
grew out of a major social movement. This is, of course, a
part of a social process. Many people believe, perhaps rightly,
that to change social attitudes it is also necessary to change
names. That is why, in the last few years, old age has been
known among students of it as "later maturity." The change
may reflect some redefinition, which, it may be, is necessary
in a country that values youth above age. (Yet it is interesting to see that gerontologists in Great Britain, where there
are more old people and where more is done for them, una-
bashedly refer to "the elderly.") Those sociologists who are
interested in action will always be tempted to redefine their
terms so as to achieve reform or save their own souls or con-
vict others of sin. He who gets into social politics would be
very stupid if he should allow himself to be a purist, insisting that all things be called by scientifically valid names
rather than by terms which mobilize people for action. But
he would be equally stupid who thought that the indiscrimi-
nate changing of names to suit his own feelings would be
effective.

If our concepts become commonly used by laymen and
acquire a burden of sentiment, they may wear out, no matter how carefully we use them. This is apparently a permanent risk in our trade. Thus far the interested public has
grasped the made-up parts of our language quickly. One
alternative is for us to make up a harder language. Some
have suggested that we turn all our concepts into letters and
signs. Such people are prejudiced against society (that means
they hate it!). It is nonsense to think that a standard terminology will put an end to the changing of meanings. Who
would check the standard terminology to see that everyone
in fact meant the same thing by the same term?

We cannot solve the problem of changing meanings by
ceasing to communicate about the things which we study,
for they are the stuff of life which people will talk about with
feeling. Since, then, it is our fate to study matters about
which people have strong sentiments, we must expect that

feelings will become entangled in the words, and develop sensitivity in detecting them.

This awareness is important for research itself, not merely for the communication of it to others. To do research we must know what we and our associates are talking about now. We must constantly ask ourselves: "What do these words mean? Why do I use them?" If we are reading research documents written by others, say a year ago, we must be sure we know what the words meant *then*. If we read a document written thirty years ago, full comprehension is almost a philological job, so rapid is the change in the connotation and denotation of terms.

A social scientist must know, too, in what mood the document was written. The historian never takes a document at its face value, nor should the sociologist; but our problem is more subtle. We have to get behind people's masks. People can deceive even more when they are talking than when they are writing. What we need, then, is both a philological understanding of the history of words and an understanding of social rhetoric, that is, of language as gestures which we make at one another. So, in sum, we must know social gestures to read documents, even if scientific; we must know them to do research ourselves, and finally, to comprehend our own thinking.

Words are weapons. As used by some people the word "Hebrew," for example, is a poisoned dart. When a word is so expressively used, we are face to face with no simple matter of social politics, but with part of the social process itself. This is, in part, what Durkheim had in mind in his long discussion of collective symbols and concepts. Words, he pointed out, are not merely something that happens along with the social process, but are its very essence. Naming is certainly part of the social process in inter-ethnic and racial relations. In contact one or the other of the groups may get renamed. Of course if the group came into being as a result of contact, it is only natural that it should get its name then. The American Negroes, as a significant social group requiring a name, were made such by the white men who brought them here and put them all into the same conditions of life. They made the group, not merely its name.

Europeans in South Africa are making a new people there. Indeed, in several parts of Africa new peoples which never existed before appear to be in the making. There will be new names, new in reference, for they will refer to new things, new groupings of men, a new spirit, a new dream of the future, new objectives; for a group becomes a people not only when they can say of themselves, "We are the people whose grandfathers came up out of Egypt," or "fought at Shiloh," or whatever it is; but when they say "We are the people who, arm in arm, are on our way to freedom," or whatever it is they want. It is not tradition alone that makes a people. It can be hope and struggle, and usually these come first. To fight and hope they must have a myth about themselves. "We, the people of the United States," was myth first, and if it refers now to a denotable reality, that is a fact of another order. The name may be a powerful, mobilizing fiction—when the name has been taken, then they can ask of a doubtful one, "Are you one of us?" This is a question which may be asked equally well in terms of the past and in terms of the future.

If an inter-ethnic relationship is at all important it will change the nature of the significant identity of the group so profoundly that it probably will need a new name. In fact, a people often needs a series of new names as interaction and redefinition go on—as it gets a new conception of itself and its fate, as it attains goals, as it gets set-backs, as it struggles on its way.

In inter-ethnic situations it is always important to ask, "Who has the naming power?"—which is not always the same as the economic and political power. Who can give a name and make it stick? And what are the references of the naming? Is it color, for instance? To illustrate:

On the eve of Indian independence Professor L. S. Ghurye, a sociologist at the University of Bombay, wrote a book to which he gave the title *The Aborigines So-Called and Their*

Future.[2] Now the name "aborigines" was one of several given by British authorities to the more or less tribal peoples of India. The general idea of the British, according to Ghurye, was to protect these people; not, of course, from British influence, but from their countrymen, the Hindus. The term "aborigines" rather suggested that the tribes were there first—just as native tribes were in Australia when the Europeans came—and that the Hindus were interlopers. This must have sounded a bit odd, coming from the British. The simple peoples of the forest ("forest tribes" was another name applied to them) were to be saved from the Hindus, but presumably not from the Christian missionaries! Another problem in naming was posed by religion: the British did not quite want to call the Hindus by a bad name, such as heathen, but they could call the tribes "animist" to indicate the more primitive state of their religions and because religion was in many cases a good way of distinguishing the tribes from castes. Anthropologists came along pretty soon and they called them "primitive tribes." The opposites of these people, by whatever name, were the Hindus, Muslims, Buddhists, and so on.

These peoples are today the problem of the government of India. Ghurye points out that the reference is no longer the imperial or colonial one of foreigner (Hindu) as against aborigine, but is the degree of integration into the larger Indian society. These peoples all believe that they raise their status if they can become a Hindu caste, even if it is only a bottom caste. Now some British observers had noticed this, of course, but thought the people foolish and perverted so to believe—how could anyone want to get into a caste system at the bottom?—and they undertook to protect them from their own folly. Naturally the government of India is not going to name them in the British way, for it sees these peoples and their aspirations in a different light; they present a problem of gradual assimilation into the national economy and body politic. Eventually there will be a new

2. Poona: The Gokhale Institute of Politics and Economics (Pub. # 11, 1943).

name for them and when it comes into being it will be a
latter-day example of a change in the reference of naming,
for the new name, we can be sure, will reflect the revolution
in political and cultural relations. Meanwhile, Ghurye
avoided the issue by using the adjective "so-called."

In the United States we might say that naming power is
in the hands of the white population, and usually of the
older, more dominant of any pair of groups. In the case of
the Negro, color was the reference. Some of the more re-
fined color terms have dropped out, as have the old names
based on supposed fractions of Negro ancestry—quadroons,
octoroons, etc. I believe Negroes themselves use color terms
with a good deal of nuance. The color question would be
solved if color no longer had any meaning but the aesthetic
—"What color of necktie will go best with my complexion?"
Sometimes the naming ignores distinctions of color. In
the early days after Pearl Harbor, when we were moving the
Americans of Japanese ancestry into "relocation camps" (a
word which under the circumstances we found much nicer
than the customary one, "concentration camp"), we needed
a name which would specify them only and set them apart
from the Japanese, Japs, "yellow bastards," etc., whom we
were fighting in the Pacific. We already had a bad conscience
about the whole business and could not bring ourselves to
call these people, who are scarcely pigmented, anyway, by a
color name, least of all "yellow." But the people themselves
had a series of names, according to the number of the generation; adult immigrants from Japan were the Issei; their
American-born children, the second generation, were the
Nisei; and the third generation were the Sansei. (The Sansei
are barely distinguishable from the Nisei and by now "Nisei"
has come to indicate all Americans of Japanese ancestry.)
We settled it by taking over their own names for themselves.
Then we began moving them out of the camps into jobs,
and that posed the persistent problem of finding a name for
ourselves, as distinguished from them. We did not want to
hurt their feelings by using a name that would imply that

they are aliens or colored, and in the end we again adopted one which the Nisei were using: Caucasians. Of course, no one seriously suggested that a Yankee, say, came from the Caucasus mountains, but the name enjoyed the great advantage of being neutral and having almost no connotations at all. The Nisei, who are notorious for going to school, probably picked it out of their geography books. However, to complete the story: we asked Dr. Tom Shibutani what name the Japanese use for us privately among themselves when they do not wish to be complimentary. It means "hairy barbarian." This is an interesting choice of symbolic trait, the more so since we, people of the hairiest race of all, use the epithet "hairy ape" to apply to supposedly lower orders of human beings.

We still call Negroes by a color name; perhaps because there is not much we can do about it, or because the Negroes have not set up new names for themselves and us. And of course, the color name is resented only because we ruined it by connotations. One suggestion has been never to mention whether a man is white or Negro, but just to forget the whole thing. If we forgot color it would be another sign that the race question no longer existed; but, if we did not mention color because it was illegal or taboo to do so, then the race question is far from solved.

The Jew—non-Jew references in naming are also perennially interesting. The Germans have almost succeeded in getting the word "Aryan" adopted as the popular opposite of Jew. They say of a person that he is "not wholly Aryan." Even if anti-Semitism were to drop to a low level in Germany this term would probably continue to be the opposite of Jewish. It is interesting to notice whether people here say "Gentile" or "Christian" when a opposite is needed. Gentile is, of course, a Latin term, while Goyim is Hebrew. Gentiles refers to the nations; that is, to those other nations. Quite logically the Mormons call the Jews with all other non-Mormons, "Gentiles."

The French Canadians often refer to themselves as "nous autres," we others. They mean, "we French Canadians recognize that we are not the main group; we are the others." To themselves the French are *les Canadiens*—the only Canadians who don't require a qualifying adjective. The others are English. Now they know very well that there are differences between English-speaking Canadians and Englishmen. The latter are *"les Anglais d'Angleterre,"* or sometimes "blokes," as the English Canadians call them. English Canadians, for their part, says "English Canadian" and "French Canadian." They admit there are two kinds.

One further dichotomy: In many European cities a working man is either a Catholic or a Socialist; or a Freethinker or Catholic. In our society the opposite of Catholic is Protestant.

Perhaps every group, even in an ideal society where people get along well with one another, has need of a private epithet for the out-groupers, as well as a public name. The line between epithet and pet-name is fine; there are affectionate epithets. To try to eliminate epithets completely is to institute a kind of thought control that may well drive thoughts and feelings to find other outlets. At any rate it is common for people to have such private names as "hairy barbarians" or as Goyim—who are, it seems, supposed to be a little stupid. Far from denying naming and trying to use it as a defense of prejudice—because it shows the objects of prejudice are themselves prejudiced—we should recognize it and go further to find out to what extent people need epithets even about people they like. For it seems to be characteristically human behavior that people do not and perhaps cannot completely accept for all purposes other people's systems of names but must have their own.

There is indeed a magic of names. It is part of our job as social scientists, and as citizens, to know how it works and when it works.

Appendix

Principle and Rationalization in Race Relations[1]

One of the most distressing and dangerous of the symptoms of our sick world is the distortion of people's minds and sentiments, and of our social practices and institutions along the axis of racial and cultural (ethnic) differences. It is right and proper that students of society should direct their attention to these symptoms and to their underlying causes. This social scientists have been and are doing. Much valuable work has been and is being done. More power to the people who are doing it; to those anthropologists who have not merely accelerated their investigations into the nature of racial differences but have also launched programs of popular education to clear up misapprehensions. All credit also to those sociologists, political scientists and other specialists who have turned their scientific effort in this direction; and to those people, of various professions, who have undertaken, by bold experiment, to bring more justice into the relations between people of different racial and ethnic backgrounds. And if scholars and other persons who are themselves members of the disadvantaged groups of our society show a special penchant for studying problems of this order, no less

1. By Everett Cherrington Hughes. A paper presented at the Eighth Annual Convention of the American Catholic Sociological Society, December 28, 1946. Reprinted from *The American Catholic Sociological Review*, VIII (March, 1947), pp. 3-11.

credit is due them. It is not only their right, but also their special duty, to undertake research and action which will benefit society at large none the less for being directed especially at injustices done to the group to which they themselves belong. The others of us in social science might, however, search our professional consciences to see whether we do not passively conspire to confine Negro social scientists to study of Negro problems, women to study of the problems of women and children, and so on (for this is one of the subtler forms of discrimination — "Go up higher, brother, to the head of your own table").

The main business of this paper is, however, not to praise, but to criticize the way in which we have gone about the business of improving the relations between races and ethnic groups.

Our main fault has been opportunism, and especially an opportunism of logic, a fault common enough in American social science and social action. I do not mean that there is necessarily any opportunism in the turning of our attention to the problems of our own time and country. On that point we should not yield an inch to those who would have us choose our objects of study purely on the basis of something called "the state of knowledge" without reference to what is currently going on in the world. There has undoubtedly been some opportunism in choice of problems for investigation by American social scientists; we may have respected sacred cows and may have run after the problems for whose investigation funds are easy to get. An opportunism of logic is, however, much more serious.

The main evidence of the kind of opportunism to which I refer is that we allow the direction of our research and educational effort to be dictated by the enemy, the defenders of racial and ethnic injustice. It is common for people to defend their sentiments and actions by rationalizations. In some societies a given set of rationalizations may last so long as to become traditional. In our society, we are quick to change them. We actively seek new ones; this is one of the functions of annual conventions — to find more up-to-date reasons for our old policies, interests and sentiments. Being scientifically minded, we Americans dress our new rationalizations in the sheep's clothing of science. The inequality in the position of the races in this country was once defended by scriptural quotation; now it is defended by what are called "facts" of biology and psychology. And those of us who are interested in getting new light on and more just action in the relations between peoples, take up the chase. If someone says Negroes have such poor jobs because they are biologically incapable of learning complicated skills, we set about to prove that Negroes can learn to do anything anyone else can learn to do. If then the "fact" of incapacity to learn is modified to say that Negroes are good with their hands, but not with their heads, we get busy to prove that that isn't so, either. Then someone comes along with the defense that although they can learn as well, or almost as well, as other people, Negroes lack sexual or other controls necessary to the nicer positions in our society; we chase that one. Or perhaps Negroes don't smell nice; so we start counting sweat glands. We store the sweat of people of various races in bottles and have it smelt by noses of several shapes, sizes and colors, just as advertising agencies say they do with cigarettes in their "scientific" blind-fold tests — and note with glee that women have more sweat-glands than men and that while the smellers couldn't tell what race the samples came from, a Chinese man picked as worst of all the sweat of an Anglo-Saxon. Someone will no doubt soon analyse the oil from the skin and hair of some group unfortunately dubbed "greasers." Perhaps some day a broad-minded East Indian will be disturbed by the disgust his fellow-countrymen are said to feel at the sight of lobster-red sunburned English skin. Desirous of eliminating this unwarranted prejudice against Europeans, he will have chemists make tests; if all goes well, they will find no chemical difference between the beautiful bronze skin of Hindu vegetarians and the parboiled hide of a beef-eating Colonel Blimp.

Now I have no basic objection to the making of such tests, and none to the dissemination, to as many people as possible, of whatever findings result from them. Truth is better than error, and should be spread with the more vigor when the error is one that does great damage. What I do object to is giving the terms of the game into the hands of the enemy, who, by inventing a new rationalization every day, leads us a merry and endless chase. We attack the devil's changing disguises instead of the devil himself.

Each of these rationalizations brought up in defense of racial and ethnic injustices is part of a syllogism. The minor premise, stating an alleged fact, is expressed; the major premise, a principle, is left out. Instead of driving our opponents and ourselves back to the major premise, we are content to question and disprove the minor premise, the allegation of fact.

Suppose we take a couple of the common statements: "Jim Crow practices are justified because Negroes smell bad," and "Jews should not be admitted to medical schools because they are aggressive." The first, completed, would read something like this:

There should be separate public facilities for people who smell bad.

Negroes smell bad.

Therefore, Negroes should have separate facilities.

The second would read like this:

People who are aggressive beyond some determined degree should not be admitted to medical schools.

Jews are aggressive beyond this degree.

Therefore, Jews should not be admitted to medical schools.

The orders of fact alleged in these two examples are quite different. But they serve equally well for our purpose. The major premise is ordinarily not stated in either case by the persons who use the statement; nor is it often stated or answered by those who oppose racial and ethnic discrimination of the kinds they refer to.

I suspect—though it might be hard to prove—that the suppression of the major premise in these and similar cases is not a psychological accident. There is said to be a kind of shrewdness in the fevered reasoning of the neurotic, as well

as in that of the devil. The shrewdness in these rationalizations lies in the use of implied major premises that people of
our culture, those who believe in racial and ethnic equality,
as well as those who use these rationalizations, do not care to
bring out into the open.

Let us look again at the syllogism about odors. We are a
people who can be frightened by advertisements which tell
us that we will not be promoted to be superintendents of
factories and sales-managers of businesses unless we smell
nice; and the American woman can be frightened by the
threat that she will not get her man or that she may lose
him over a matter of a little unpleasant odor of which her
best friend can't bring herself to speak. We are not told at
what point in his rise to authority and higher income the
man must begin to make himself pleasant. Nor do we learn
whether the man who is about to be lost had so sensitive a
nose when he got the girl, or whether he picked up this
nicety later. But the reference to the great—and legitimate—
American dream of getting ahead is obvious enough. And it
is perhaps not difficult to understand why we do not question the main premise behind the alleged fact of Negro odor.

Or let us take the defense of restrictive covenants by the
statement that the presence of Negroes in a neighborhood
destroys property values. The major premise would be something like this: People are justified in preventing property
in their neighborhood from being occupied by people whose
presence reduces property values. Now it is true that residential property values respond in some degree, under certain circumstances, to a change in the kind of people who
live in the area. This may be due to the way of living of the
new people, or it may be due to an attitude toward them,
or to both. It is also true that Americans in great numbers
try to turn an improvement in their economic condition
into an improvement in their social standing by moving to
a new neighborhood. This is a perfectly natural and generally proper thing for them to do. But the trouble is that
there is always some later comer treading on one's heels. So
that it is, in a sense, the great American game to break in

where one is not wanted. It is a game that is successful just
to the extent that one seems not to be playing it: to seem to
play it is to be aggressive, and one gets punished for that although he may not necessarily be rewarded for not being aggressive. Herein lies the great American dilemma, although
I do not mean to belittle Mr. Myrdal's statement of it. The
thought that I may be one of those whose presence in a
neighborhood might—through other people's attitudes toward me—reduce its desirability to them is not a pleasant
one to face, especially when combined with my own concern
lest some group of people from whom I wish to be dissociated
may some day threaten the neighborhood in which I have
achieved a social footing and perhaps a dearly bought family
house.

The preceding paragraph contains a clue to the effectiveness of the use of alleged Jewish aggressiveness as justification
for limiting their entry to the professions. We Americans
do not like to talk about just what degree of aggressiveness is proper; we might find that the amount of this
virtue necessary to realize our ambitions is greater than the
amount which turns it into a punishable vice. I am tempted
to pursue a like analysis of what is hidden in the question,
"How would you like your sister to marry a nigger?" I will
spare you—and myself—that ordeal. To those of you who are
still college students, I recommend it as an exercise for the
brain and the spine.

Let me repeat that I do not pretend to prove that the ene-
mies of interracial and interethnic justice exercise conscious
slyness in the choice of their defensive rationalizations. Nor
can I prove that it is the discomfort of facing major premises
about which we are fearfully ambivalent, rather than mere
logical carelessness and the love of empiricism at all costs,
that prevents us from filling out these syllogisms. But certainly we are ambivalent about the principles hidden in these
statements. We, like those who defend the racial and ethnic
inequalities of our society, are all Americans. They and we
share the same aspirations; the hidden fundament of our
minds is the same as theirs. I only suggest that that gives

them a certain advantage over us, and that we have allowed them full benefit of it.[2]

Whatever causes it, the failure to ferret out major premises has other consequences than merely leading us on to a merry chase for facts. It leads to too much protestation as well. We counter the exaggerated statements of our opponents with exaggerations in another direction. Nearly all of the statements in favor of racial and ethnic discrimination allege faults in the minority groups in question. These faults range from serious moral defect to slight departures from the canons of good taste. In our counter-arguments, the members of the racial or ethnic groups involved appear as paragons of virtue, delightful in their manners—better, in fact, than it is common for human creatures to be.

This brings up the whole problem of the differences between people of different racial and ethnic categories. Those opposed to racial prejudices and inequalities have shown a tendency to slight, or even to deny, the existence of any differences at all. Fishberg's book on the Jews has long served as a text to prove that no one can tell a Jew when he sees him—a very dubious compliment to Jewish parents who have put forth great effort so to bring up their children that they will respect and practice conduct which the parents consider rooted in their Jewish faith and culture. All that Fishberg says about the physical characteristics of Jews may be true; and there are occasions when statement of his or other such findings is called for. But to use them to try to prove that there are no discernible or significant differences between one ethnic, or religious, group and another can lead to no good.

In the first place, overuse of such argument implies that the only basis for social, political and economic equality is the lack of differences between the groups concerned. That would put our faith in the rightness of social equality on a very dubious foundation, both because it might some day

---

2. For a penetrating analysis of hidden factors in interethnic sentiment, see Ichheiser, Gustav, "Diagnosis of Anti-Semitism," *Sociometry Monographs*, No. 8.

turn out that there are some differences we don't know about and because it would imply that the price of equality is the elimination of peculiar traits which some group of people may properly cultivate and cherish. Heaven knows that in our prejudiced world members of some groups are given plenty of temptation to deny that they belong to the groups in which they were born and bred, and in so doing to eliminate all identifying marks. That is a matter for their own consciences. We can only have sympathy for such victims of racial, ethnic and religious injustice. Our sympathy should not lead us to engage in counter-propaganda which expressly or implicitly denies or tones down the differences which really exist between groups.

There is, further, the danger—so cogently stated by David Riesman in an article entitled "Equality and Social Structure,"—that common people will consider the whole propaganda for tolerance a fake intended to obfuscate them. For, as Riesman says—speaking of the way into which the democratic world played into the hands of the Nazis—

That (democratic) world denied that there was any difference between races. . . . [Anthropologists] insisted . . . that only the ignorant and the prejudiced could find any differences between Jews and non-Jews, and sociologists supplemented this with statistics to show that, in all tangible ways, Jews were just like everybody else. . . . One can see now that it would have been better strategy to admit the differences while denying that they justified political and economic stratification in most cases. . . . For the differences *are* there, no less so for being subtle and impalpable, or being mostly culturally conditioned, not biological in origin. . . .

At any rate, in the eyes of the ordinary man, there were differences between races and between the sexes and between men in general. He could not always put his finger on them, but he could feel them, and feel that there was something fishy in the liberal denials.[3]

Riesman's warning applies not only to those differences which merely distinguish, or are supposed to, one group from

3. *Journal of Legal and Political Sociology*, Vol. I, 1943, pp. 79-80.

another; it applies as well to those real or alleged differences which imply faults. For if groups of people maintain somewhat different virtues in their peculiar cultures, is it not likely that they will differ somewhat in their vices also? A record of the problems with which practical theologians have had to deal in different times and places, and of the special questions of conscience which have turned up in the confessional in various periods and countries, and among people of different ethnic background and social position, would— I am sure—give ample evidence of differences in the sins for which people have a predilection. In this matter, it would probably be more effective to gloss over nothing; and especially not to gloss over our own sins. The doctrine of original sin, which rests equally on all, is a sounder starting point than protestation that the groups which are the special objects of prejudice do not have any special vices. For, again speaking of our logical opportunism, the use of the denial of special faults as an argument against racial or ethnic prejudices and injustices implies somehow that we who are not discriminated against are in that blessed state because at some time or other we were without special disqualifying faults or vices, and were therefore elevated to our privileged position. It further implies the right of those who consider themselves without special faults or vices to give or withhold full equality from others.

In this kind of argument, incidentally, we again play into the hands of the enemy, for in arguing so hard that groups of people whose rights we have limited are without fault we encourage the idea—implicit in the "fault" justification of prejudice and limited rights—that justice and equality are something to be earned, and that the wage is to be paid by and at the discretion of the more privileged group. This argument turns up in the statement that Negroes are not ready for full political rights and for access to all kinds of jobs, supported by a false use of evolutionary ideas—"the Negroes are only yesterday out of the jungle." "It will take another hundred years," etc.

I do not mean to suggest that the problem of the relation

between faults and access to full privileges in a society is an easy one, either in theory or in practice. There are circumstances in which society withdraws full freedom from an individual because of a weakness betrayed in his actions towards others. But the principle on which this is done is not that the other members of society have the right to do this because they are virtuous. They do it not in the name of and by right of their own virtue, but in the name of the good of the community and through functionaries of the law who—although they should certainly be people of uprightness and as far above reproach as possible—act with an authority delegated by society. The principles involved are far from those implied in any rationalization which justifies one group of people, supposedly free of faults, in limiting the social privileges of another whole category of persons because of the latter's alleged faults. It is some such principle that we give consent to if we answer the "fault" argument for discrimination by protesting that the minority concerned is not different in any way from other groups. It makes us parties to a revolting self-righteousness.

Allow me to mention briefly one more consequence of the denial or glossing over of differences, and especially of faults. It has already led to a feeling, in this country, that no one not a member of a certain group may express any but the most laudatory sentiments or judgments concerning it. Even those who are members of a group are enjoined to say nothing critical in such a way that it may reach ears outside the group. Again, the abuses and misunderstandings have been so flagrant that one can understand the effort to enforce a certain censorship upon criticism of one group by members of another. But that kind of tolerance which prevents statement of honest opinion and conviction is a false tolerance. It is the kind of tolerance which requires us to look about the room, and ask of our neighbor in a whisper, "Is there a Lower Slobbovian present?" before we open our mouths to speak. Granting that a careful tongue is an organ of great virtue, it does not follow that an honest one is less to be valued.

I have made but one point, or sung but one theme, with some variations: that it is worse than of no avail to gather and disseminate the true facts which refute the alleged facts offered in defense of racial and ethnic inequality of social rights, unless at the same time we dig out and bring to our own view, as well as to that of our opponents, the major premises, or principles, which lie hidden beneath the disguise of rationalizations.

The Study of Ethnic Relations [4]

Since so many people are making a desperate effort (perhaps the last before they meet their Maker) to understand and modify the relations between peoples, ethnic groups and races, it is appropriate to note some of the biases and false assumptions that vitiate well-intentioned study and discussion of these relations. The relations between French and other Canadians are not one of the desperate cases. Quite the contrary. The points I have to make, however, apply to the Canadian case as well as to those that threaten the peace of the world.

I have already used the term *ethnic group,* a colorless catch-all much used by anthropologists and sociologists; it is a term likely to be taken up by a larger public, and consequently likely to take on color that will compel the sociologists to get a new one, for it is one of the risks of our trade that our words lose the scientifically essential virtue of neutrality as they acquire the highly desirable virtue of being commonly used. The anthropologists probably will not have to change, since they study people who cannot read. To return from this digression, which does have a point for the

4. By Everett Cherrington Hughes. Reprinted from *The Dalhousie Review,* XXVII, no. 4 (January, 1948), pp. 477-82.

subject in hand: what is an ethnic group? Almost anyone who uses the term would say that it is a group distinguishable from others by one, or some combination of the following: physical characteristics, language, religion, customs, institutions, or "cultural traits." This definition is, however, exactly wrong-end to. Its wrongness has important consequences, not only for study of inter-group relations, but for the relations themselves. An ethnic group is not one because of the degree of measurable or observable difference from other groups; it is an ethnic group, on the contrary, because the people in it and the people out of it know that it is one; because both the *ins* and the *outs* talk, feel and act as if it were a separate group. This is possible only if there are ways of telling who belongs to the group and who does not, and if a person learns early, deeply, and usually irrevocably to what group he belongs. If it is easy to resign from the group, it is not truly an ethnic group.

These points should be clear and dear to any English-speaking Canadian. By the kind of measures usually used, the English-speaking part of the Canadian people would be considered a colony of Great Britain or a part of the United States. About all the evidence to prove that Canadians are a separate ethnic group is a little extra virtue and the fact that they export their Aimee Semple McPhersons, Tex Guinans, Norma Shearers, Pidgeons and Masseys—and buy them back at the box-office. Yet Canadians are Canadians just as naturally as Englishmen are Englishmen, and they never yield to the temptation to belong to other nations. Well, hardly ever.

To be sure, the living of a common life and the facing of common problems—conditions that lead to the growth of an ethnic group, nationality and even a race—will almost certainly encourage the development of a peculiar language, at least of peculiar turns of expression and meaning, and of some unique customs and institutions. Some of these peculiar traits will become the dear symbols of the group's distinction from others; their value for group solidarity may exceed their measurable degree of uniqueness. The essential fact remains, however, that the cultural traits are attributes of the group, and not that the group is the synthesis of its traits.

What difference does this error make? It warps study both of groups and also of the relations between them. When I first went from Chicago to McGill University, I took with me the conventional notions of studying the assimilation and acculturation (to use both the sociologists' and the anthropologists' lingo) of European immigrants in North America. I looked up all the studies I could find of what was happening to the French Canadians. In the census I sought figures on the number of French Canadians who speak English. Now the assumption was that French Canadians are being gradually assimilated to the English-Canadian culture and world, and that the trait of language was the index thereof. If a French Canadian spoke English, he was presumably less French. It took me a long time to discover that the French Canadian who speaks English best is generally pretty stoutly French in sentiment and way of living, and that sometimes one who speaks but little English has often suffered severe lesions in the integrity of his French culture and loyalty. Eventually I learned that one of the commonest errors of English Canadians is to take the use of English, a tweed coat, or something else considered an expression of Englishness, as evidence that some French Canadian they meet is about to resign from his group. Later, when they discover that he is more French than they have thought, they decide he has reverted. In fact, the English Canadians have simply learned more about him. A certain withdrawal of cordiality often results. The misunderstanding arises from the error of considering that individual cultural traits are the measure of a man's belonging to an ethnic group, and of the solidarity of the group itself. This error is usually accompanied by the hidden assumption that the individual traits are, or ought to be, disappearing and that one fine day they will be gone—and the French-Canadian people will no longer exist. This is misjudgment, of course, in line with the common tendency to regard one's own group as immortal and the other as relatively a passing thing. It might, incidentally, be interesting to speculate upon what will have become of English Canadians as an ethnic entity by the time French Canadians have disappeared as one.

An additional consequence or expression (I will not try to be too nice about deciding which) of this point of view is the judging of a group's right to exist on the basis of the quality of its cultural peculiarities, called for this purpose "cultural contributions." An English-Canadian teacher of French in a Canadian university used to maintain—in a stout Ontario twang—that since French Canadians had corrupted the French language into a "patois" and since they had made no worthy contributions to French literature and culture, they had no right to hold out from the English-Canadian language and culture. This argument could cut both ways. Whether in the Canadian case it cuts either way is not an issue. Before deciding the case of any people, one would have to agree upon some canons of linguistic and literary aesthetics and upon some standards by which to determine when a contribution to culture has been made. Need I dwell upon the difficulty of getting such agreement from people of two cultures?

Thus far I have myself contributed to another and graver error, that of implying that one can study the relations between groups by analyzing only one of the groups concerned. It takes more than one ethnic group to make ethnic relations. The relations can be no more understood by studying one or the other of the groups than can a chemical combination by study of one element only, or a boxing bout by observation of only one of the fighters. Yet it is common to study ethnic relations as if one had to know only one party to them. Generally the person who studies such relations is a member of one of the groups involved. One might suppose that he would assume that he knows his own group and would therefore study the other. That is not quite what happens. Most studies turn out to deal mainly with whichever of the groups is considered the minority. The student who is himself of the minority wants to make his group known and appreciated by the dominant group; one who is of the dominant group is likely to assume that he knows his own and that the problem is, after all, one of how the minority will adjust to the dominant group. In conducting a seminar on race and cultural contacts, I have found that the majority of students propose projects that are simply studies of some minority group, with the word *problem* attached: the Nisei problem, the Flemish problem, the French-Canadian problem. In the resulting reports, the dominant group gets off with a drubbing because of its prejudices, although it may be shown that there is hope of a more "liberal" attitude's arising in some hearts. The wounds and virtues of the minority are exposed to view and their relics to veneration. The *relations,* however, are never studied. Since it is generally true that members of a minority have a more lively experience of the dominant group than members of the latter have of the minority, more can perhaps be learned about the inter-group relations by studying the minority than by studying the dominant group. This might give some justification for starting with the minority, but not for leaving the matter there, as is often done. Even that would not be so bad, if the study were pushed into all realms of life and experience, and not limited to political and economic relations. Much is to be learned about inter-group relations by probing to the depths of personal experience, by discovering through what experiences the individual learns both the realities and the fictions of his position as a member of an ethnic group. To what literature can one turn to study this aspect of French-English relations in Canada?

But whether a student studies one or all the groups in a situation—and he should study all—he must study *relations* if that is what he claims he wants to know. If he puts the emphasis on relations, he will find out fairly easily what kind of things he will have to know about the groups themselves in order to understand the relations. He will learn, for instance, that study of folklore, as such, is not study of inter-group relations; but he will also become sensitive to the hints of group loyalty and aggression in tales and songs. He will sit up and listen to a French-Canadian folksong in which, long ago, the rich old man whom the pretty young maid does not want to marry was turned into a *maudit anglais*. He will turn to the folklorist, who will be able to tell him more of the history of the song and who will correct his impressions— as one of the several excellent French-Canadian folklorists will probably do to my interpretation of the above song. He will also learn, however, to discipline his own passion for curio- and antique-hunting by keeping his eye firmly on the objective of studying relations. He will find his curiosity about both groups greatly enlivened and his eye sharpened, but he will not try to be a specialist in all matters concerning the group and will turn willingly to others for their specialized knowledge.

Now the way to keep this disciplining objective in mind is to start quite consciously with an assumption; namely, that if the groups in question have enough relations to be a nuisance to each other it is because they form a part of a whole, that they are in some sense and in some measure members of the same body. With this idea firmly in mind, one can set about finding out what the whole is and what is the part of each in the whole. In doing this, one will almost certainly not fall into the errors so far considered, and will avoid another one: that of studying only the conscious surface of the relations between groups—their quarrels, opinions, propaganda and counter-propaganda. Among the respects in which the two groups are parts of a larger whole may be some of which people are not ordinarily aware and of which, if they are aware of them, they do not ordinarily think in ethnic terms at all. This conception will also keep one from thinking that either of the groups has so independent an existence that it could be studied without reference to other groups around it.

Almost anyone will agree that the French-Canadian people has become what it is, not merely by virtue of what its ancestors brought with them from France, but also because of its long contact with Anglo-American life and civilization. I refer not to anglicisms in its speech, its love of baseball, or other English or North American customs which it may have adopted, but to its very peculiarities. French Canada has never had to swallow its own spit. Its balance of population has long been maintained by spilling the excess into a continent until recently thirsty for settlers and industrial labor. Its malcontents and heretics have been able to find companions and a place to exercise their peculiar talents somewhere in North America. How much relief from inner pressure of number and of psychological and social tension French Canada has been afforded by being part of something much larger than herself, no one can say. Nor can I prove, although I think it is so, that the failure of the continent to continue this function of absorption for French Canada is partly responsible for the current brand of more bitter nationalism and nationalist in Quebec.

I stress the functions that the rest of Canada and North America perform for Quebec, not to reinforce any feelings that other Canadians may have about French Canada's debt to the English-speaking world, but to prepare for the kill. There has been some study of the economic, demographic, and political functions of French Canada in the development of Canada as a whole, but not much of her cultural and deeper psychological functions in the development of the rest of the Canadian people. During the war, the two-thirds vote of French Canadians against conscription served beautifully to obscure the one-third vote of other Canadians against it. In those years, I frequently heard my United States compatriots most unjustly and ignorantly criticize the magnificent Canadian war effort. How often I heard English Canadians, instead of answering with the eloquent facts, defensively impugn the patriotism of their French-Canadian fellow citizens! The temptation was great. Indeed, the critic often suggested this way out himself, since he usually wanted to think well of the Canadian. Proving oneself a good fellow on the other fellow's terms, however, does not generally increase the other fellow's respect for the group to which one belongs; and in this case it may be doubted whether Canada was well served. The presence of a minority whose sentiments vary from one's own, either in direction or intensity, is a wonderful salve to the conscience. If one wear the salve thickly and conspicuously enough, who shall dare question whether there is really a wound under it? Just what the fact of having always had a minority in its bosom has done to the national conscience and self-consciousness of English Canadians is worth study. I offer this very controversial point, like others in this paper, as bait to those who would explore the full depth and subtlety of the effects upon each other of two ethnic groups who are parts of a larger whole. Note, too, that in pushing the conception of the relations between two groups so far, we have gone beyond the effort to be merely impartial and just. Impartial judgment implies a standard of justice, legal and moral. This is precisely what two groups are least likely to agree upon, especially in a crisis.

I plead, however, not for less justice of word and action between ethnic groups, races and peoples, but for a more drastically objective, a broader and more penetrating, analysis with which to work.

Dilemmas and Contradictions of Status [5]

It is doubtful whether any society ever had so great a variety of statuses or recognized such a large number of status-determining characteristics as does ours. The combinations of the latter are, of course, times over more numerous than the characteristics themselves. In societies where statuses [6] are well defined and are entered chiefly by birth or a few

---

5. By Everett Cherrington Hughes. Reprinted from *The American Journal of Sociology*, L, no. 5 (March 1945), pp. 353-9.

6. "Status" is here taken in its strict sense as a defined social position for whose incumbents there are defined rights, limitations of rights, and duties. See the *Oxford Dictionary* and any standard Latin lexicon. Since statuses tend to form a hierarchy, the term itself has—since Roman times—had the additional meaning of rank.

well-established sequences of training or achievement, the particular personal attributes proper to each status are woven into a whole. They are not thought of as separate entities. Even in our society, certain statuses have developed characteristic patterns of expected personal attributes and a way of life. To such, in the German language, is applied the term *Stand.*

Few of the positions in our society, however, have remained fixed long enough for such an elaboration to occur. We put emphasis on change in the system of positions which make up our social organization and upon mobility of the individual by achievement. In the struggle for achievement, individual traits of the person stand out as separate entities. And they occur in peculiar combinations which make for confusion, contradictions, and dilemmas of status.

I shall, in this paper, elaborate the notion of contradictions and dilemmas of status. Illustrations will be taken from professional and other occupational positions. The idea was put into a suggestive phrase by Robert E. Park when he wrote of the "marginal man." He applied the term to a special kind of case—the racial hybrid—who, as a consequence of the fact that races have become defined as status groups, finds himself in a status dilemma.

Now there may be, for a given status or social position, one or more specifically determining characteristics of the person. Some of them are formal, or even legal. No one, for example, has the status of physician unless he be duly licensed. A foreman is not such until appointed by proper authority. The heavy soprano is not a prima donna in more than temperament until formally cast for the part by the director of the opera. For each of these particular positions there is also an expected technical competence. Neither the formal nor the technical qualifications are, in all cases, so clear. Many statuses, such as membership in a social class, are not determined in a formal way. Other statuses are ill-defined both as to the characteristics which determine identification with them and as to their duties and rights.

There tends to grow up about a status, in addition to its

specifically determining traits, a complex of auxiliary characteristics which come to be expected of its incumbents. It seems entirely natural to Roman Catholics that all priests should be men, although piety seems more common among women. In this case the expectation is supported by formal rule. Most doctors, engineers, lawyers, professors, managers and supervisors in industrial plants are men, although no law requires that they be so. If one takes a series of characteristics, other than medical skill and a license to practice it, which individuals in our society may have, and then thinks of physicians possessing them in various combinations, it becomes apparent that some of the combinations seem more natural and are more acceptable than others to the great body of potential patients. Thus a white, male, Protestant physician of old American stock and of a family of at least moderate social standing would be acceptable to patients of almost any social category in this country. To be sure, a Catholic might prefer a physician of his own faith for reasons of spiritual comfort. A few ardent feminists, a few race-conscious Negroes, a few militant sectarians, might follow their principles to the extent of seeking a physician of their own category. On the other hand, patients who identify themselves with the "old stock" may, in an emergency, take the first physician who turns up.[7]

If the case is serious, patients may seek a specialist of some strange or disliked social category, letting the reputation for special skill override other traits. The line may be crossed

----

7. A Negro physician, driving through northern Indiana, came upon a crowd standing around a man just badly injured in a road accident. The physician tended the man and followed the ambulance which took him to the hospital. The hospital authorities tried to prevent the physician from entering the hospital for even long enough to report to staff physicians what he had done for the patient. The same physician, in answer to a Sunday phone call asking him to visit a supposedly very sick woman, went to a house. When the person who answered the door saw that the physician was a Negro, she insisted that they had not called for a doctor and that no one in the house was sick. When he insisted on being paid, the people in the house did so, thereby revealing their lie. In the first instance, an apparently hostile crowd accepted the Negro as a physician because of urgency. In the second, he was refused presumably because the emergency was not great enough.

also when some physician acquires such renown that his office becomes something of a shrine, a place of wonderful, last-resort cures. Even the color line is not a complete bar to such a reputation. On the contrary, it may add piquancy to the treatment of a particularly enjoyed malady or lend hope to the quest for a cure of an "incurable" ailment. Allowing for such exceptions, it remains probably true that the white, male, Protestant physician of old American stock, although he may easily fail to get a clientele at all, is categorically acceptable to a greater variety of patients than is he who departs, in one or more particulars, from this type.

It is more exact to say that, if one were to imagine patients of the various possible combinations of these same characteristics (race, sex, religion, ethnic background, family standing), such a physician could treat patients of any of the resulting categories without a feeling by the physician, patient, or the surrounding social circle that the situation was unusual or shocking. One has only to make a sixteen-box table showing physicians of the possible combinations of race (white and Negro) and sex with patients of the possible combinations to see that the white male is the only resulting kind of physician to whom patients of all the kinds are completely accessible in our society (see Table 1).

TABLE 1 *

PATIENT	PHYSICIAN			
	White Male	White Female	Negro Male	Negro Female
White male	....	....	....	....
White female	....	....	....	....
Negro male	....	....	....	....
Negro female	....	....	....	....

* I have not used this table in any study of preferences but should be glad if anyone interested were to do so with selected groups of people.

One might apply a similar analysis to situations involving other positions, such as the foreman and the worker, the teacher and the pupil. Each case may be complicated by adding other categories of persons with whom the person of the given position has to deal. The teacher, in practice, has dealings not only with pupils but with parents, school boards, other public functionaries, and, finally, his own colleagues. Immediately one tries to make this analysis, it becomes clear that a characteristic which might not interfere with some of the situations of a given position may interfere with others.

I do not maintain that any considerable proportion of people do consciously put together in a systematic way their expectations of persons of given positions. I suggest, rather, that people carry in their minds a set of expectations concerning the auxiliary traits properly associated with many of the specific positions available in our society. These expectations appear as advantages or disadvantages to persons who, in keeping with American social belief and practice, aspire to positions new to persons of their kind.

The expected or "natural" combinations of auxiliary characteristics become embodied in the stereotypes of ordinary talk, cartoons, fiction, the radio, and the motion picture. Thus, the American Catholic priest, according to a popular stereotype, is Irish, athletic, and a good sort who with difficulty refrains from profanity in the presence of evil and who may punch someone in the nose if the work of the Lord demands it. Nothing could be farther from the French or French-Canadian stereotype of the good priest. The surgeon, as he appears in advertisements for insurance and pharmaceutical products, is handsome, socially poised, and young of face but gray about the temples. These public, or publicity, stereotypes—while they do not necessarily correspond to the facts or determine people's expectations—are at least significant in that they rarely let the person in the given position have any strikes against him. Positively, they represent someone's ideal conception; negatively, they take care not to shock, astonish, or put doubts into the mind of a public whose confidence is sought.

If we think especially of occupational status, it is in the colleague-group or fellow-worker group that the expectations concerning appropriate auxiliary characteristics are worked most intricately into sentiment and conduct. They become, in fact, the basis of the colleague-group's definition of its common interests, of its informal code, and of selection of those who become the inner fraternity—three aspects of occupational life so closely related that few people separate them in thought or talk.

The epithets "hen doctor," "boy wonder," "bright young men," and "brain trust" express the hostility of colleagues to persons who deviate from the expected type. The members of a colleague-group have a common interest in the whole configuration of things which control the number of potential candidates for their occupation. Colleagues, be it remembered, are also competitors. A rational demonstration that an individual's chances for continued success are not jeopardized by an extension of the recruiting field for the position he has or hopes to attain, or by some short-cutting of usual lines of promotion, does not, as a rule, liquidate the fear and hostility aroused by such a case. Oswald Hall found that physicians do not like one of their number to become a consultant too soon.[8] Consulting is something for the crowning, easing-off years of a career; something to intervene briefly between high power and high blood-pressure. He who pushes for such practice too early shows an "aggressiveness" which is almost certain to be punished. It is a threat to an order of things which physicians—at least, those of the fraternity of successful men—count upon. Many of the specific rules of the game of an occupation become comprehensible only when viewed as the almost instinctive attempts of a group of people to cushion themselves against the hazards of their careers. The advent of colleague-competitors of some new and peculiar type, or by some new route, is likely to arouse anxieties. For one thing, one cannot be quite sure how "new people"—new in kind—will act in the various contingencies which arise to test the solidarity of the group.[9]

8. Oswald Hall, "The Informal Organization of Medical Practice" (unpublished Ph.D. dissertation, University of Chicago, 1944).

9. It may be that those whose positions are insecure and whose hopes for the higher goals are already fading express more violent hostility to "new

How the expectations of which we are thinking become embodied in codes may be illustrated by the dilemma of a young woman who became a member of that virile profession, engineering. The designer of an airplane is expected to go up on the maiden flight of the first plane built according to the design. He (*sic*) then gives a dinner to the engineers and workmen who worked on the new plane. The dinner is naturally a stag party. The young woman in question designed a plane. Her co-workers urged her not to take the risk—for which, presumably, men only are fit—of the maiden voyage. They were, in effect, asking her to be a lady rather than an engineer. She chose to be an engineer. She then gave the party and paid for it like a man. After the food and the first round of toasts, she left like a lady.

Part of the working code of a position is discretion; it allows the colleagues to exchange confidences concerning their relations to other people. Among these confidences one finds expressions of cynicism concerning their mission, their competence, and the foibles of their superiors, themselves, their clients, their subordinates, and the public at large. Such expressions take the burden from one's shoulders and serve as a defense as well. The unspoken mutual confidence necessary to them rests on two assumptions concerning one's fellows. The first is that the colleague will not misunderstand; the second is that he will not repeat to uninitiated ears. To be sure that a new fellow will not misunderstand requires a sparring match of social gestures. The zealot who turns the sparring match into a real battle, who takes a friendly initiation too seriously, is not likely to be trusted with the lighter sort of comment on one's work or with doubts and misgivings; nor can he learn those parts of the working code which are communicated only by hint and gesture. He is not to be trusted, for, though he is not fit for stratagems, he is suspected of being prone to treason. In order that men may communicate freely and confidentially, they must be able to take a

---

people." Even if so, it must be remembered that those who are secure and successful have the power to exclude or check the careers of such people by merely failing to notice them.

good deal of each other's sentiments for granted. They must feel easy about their silences as well as about their utterances. These factors conspire to make colleagues with a large body of unspoken understandings uncomfortable in the presence of what they consider odd kinds of fellows. The person who is the first of his kind to attain a certain status is often not drawn into the informal brotherhood in which experiences are exchanged, competence built up, and the formal code elaborated and enforced. He thus remains forever a marginal man.

Now it is a necessary consequence of the high degree of individual mobility in America that there should be large numbers of people of new kinds turning up in various positions. In spite of this and in spite of American heterogeneity, this remains a white, Anglo-Saxon, male, Protestant culture in many respects. These are the expected characteristics for many favored statuses and positions. When we speak of racial, religious, sex, and ethnic prejudices, we generally assume that people with these favored qualities are not the objects thereof. In the stereotyped prejudices concerning others, there is usually contained the assumption that these other people are peculiarly adapted to the particular places which they have held up to the present time; it is a corollary implication that they are not quite fit for new positions to which they may aspire. In general, advance of a new group—women, Negroes, some ethnic groups, etc.—to a new level of positions is not accompanied by complete disappearance of such stereotypes but only by some modification of them. Thus, in Quebec the idea that French Canadians were good only for unskilled industrial work was followed by the notion that they were especially good at certain kinds of skilled work but were not fit to repair machines or to supervise the work of others. In this series of modifications the structure of qualities expected for the most-favored positions remains intact. But the forces which make for mobility continue to create marginal people on new frontiers.

Technical changes also break up configurations of expected status characteristics by altering the occupations about which they grow up. A new machine or a new managerial device—such as the assembly line—may create new positions or break old ones up into numbers of new ones. The length of training may be changed thereby and, with it, the whole traditional method of forming the person to the social demands of a colleague-group. Thus, a slip of a girl is trained in a few weeks to be a "machinist" on a practically foolproof lathe; thereby the old foolproof machinist, who was initiated slowly into the skills and attitudes of the trade, is himself made a fool of in his own eyes or—worse—in the eyes of his wife, who hears that a neighbor's daughter is a machinist who makes nearly as much money as he. The new positions created by technical changes may, for a time, lack definition as a status. Both the technical and the auxiliary qualifications may be slow in taking form. The personnel man offers a good example. His title is perhaps twenty years old but the expectations concerning his qualities and functions are still in flux.[10]

Suppose we leave aside the problems which arise from technical changes, as such, and devote the rest of this discussion to the consequences of the appearance of new kinds of people in established positions. Every such occurence produces, in some measure, a status contradiction. It may also create a status dilemma for the individual concerned and for other people who have to deal with him.

The most striking illustration in our society is offered by the Negro who qualifies for one of the traditional professions. Membership in the Negro race, as defined in American mores and/or law, may be called a master status-determining trait. It tends to overpower, in most crucial situations, any other characteristics which might run counter to it. But profes-

---

10. The personnel man also illustrates another problem which I do not propose to discuss in this paper. It is that of an essential contradiction between the various functions which are united in one position. The personnel man is expected to communicate the mind of the workers to management and then to interpret management to the workers. This is a difficult assignment. The problem is well stated by William F. Whyte, in "Pity the Personnel Man," *Advanced Management*, October-December, 1944, pp. 154-58. The Webbs analyzed the similar dilemma of the official of a successful trade-union in their *History of Trade-Unionism* (rev. ed.; London: Longmans, Green, 1920).

sional standing is also a powerful characteristic—most so in the specific relationships of professional practice, less so in the general intercourse of people. In the person of the professionally qualified Negro these two powerful characteristics clash. The dilemma, for those whites who meet such a person, is that of having to choose whether to treat him as a Negro or as a member of his profession.

The white person in need of professional services, especially medical, might allow a Negro physician to act as doctor in an emergency. Or it may be allowed that he is endowed with some uncanny skill. In either case, the white client of ordinary American social views would probably avoid any nonprofessional contacts with the Negro physician.[11] In fact, one way of reducing status conflict is to keep the relationship formal and specific. This is best done by walking through a door into a place designed for the specific relationship, a door which can be firmly closed when one leaves. A common scene in fiction depicts a lady of degree seeking, veiled and alone, the address of the fortuneteller or the midwife of doubtful practice in an obscure corner of the city. The anonymity of certain sections of cities allows people to seek specialized services, legitimate but embarassing as well as illegitimate, from persons with whom they would not want to be seen by members of their own social circle.

Some professional situations lend themselves more than others to such quarantine. The family physician and the pediatrician cannot be so easily isolated as some other specialists. Certain legal services can be sought indirectly by being delegated to some queer and unacceptable person by the family lawyer. At the other extreme is school teaching, which is done in full view of the community and is generally expected to be accompanied by an active role in community undertakings. The teacher, unlike the lawyer, is expected to be an example to her charges.

---

11. The Negro artist can be treated as a celebrity. It is within the code of social tufthunting that one may entertain, with a kind of affected Bohemian intimacy, celebrities who, on all counts other than their artistic accomplishments, would be beyond the pale.

For the white colleagues of the Negro professional man the dilemma is even more severe. The colleague-group is ideally a brotherhood; to have within it people who cannot, given one's other attitudes, be accepted as brothers is very uncomfortable. Furthermore, professional men are much more sensitive than they like to admit about the company in which nonprofessionals see them. The dilemma arises from the fact that, while it is bad for the profession to let laymen see rifts in their ranks, it may be bad for the individual to be associated in the eyes of his actual or potential patients with persons, even colleagues, of so despised a group as the Negro. The favored way of avoiding the dilemma is to shun contacts with the Negro professional. The white physician or surgeon of assured reputation may solve the problem by acting as consultant to Negro colleagues in Negro clinics and hospitals.

For the Negro professional man there is also a dilemma. If he accepts the role of Negro to the extent of appearing content with less than full equality and intimacy with his white colleagues, for the sake of such security and advantage as can be so got, he himself and others may accuse him of sacrificing his race. Given the tendency of whites to say that any Negro who rises to a special position is an exception, there is a strong temptation for such a Negro to seek advantage by fostering the idea that he is unlike others of his race. The devil who specializes in this temptation is a very insinuating fellow; he keeps a mailing list of "marginal men" of all kinds and origins. Incidentally, one of the by-products of American mores is the heavy moral burden which this temptation puts upon the host of Americans who have by great effort risen from (*sic*) groups which are the objects of prejudice.

There may be cases in which the appearance in a position of one or a few individuals of a kind not expected there immediately dissolves the auxiliary expectations which make him appear odd. This is not, however, the usual consequence. The expectations usually continue to exist, with modifications and with exceptions allowed.

A common solution is some elaboration of social segregation. The woman lawyer may become a lawyer to women clients, or she may specialize in some kind of legal service in keeping with woman's role as guardian of the home and of morals. Women physicians may find a place in those specialities of which only women and children have need. A female electrical engineer was urged by the dean of the school from which she had just been graduated to accept a job whose function was to give the "woman's angle" to design of household electrical appliances. The Negro professional man finds his clients among Negroes. The Negro sociologist generally studies race relations and teaches in a Negro college. A new figure on the American scene is the Negro personnel man in industries which have started employing Negro workers. His functions are to adjust difficulties of Negro workers, settle minor clashes between the races, and to interpret management's policies to the Negro as well as to present and explain the Negro's point of view to management. It is a difficult job. Our interest for the moment, however, is in the fact that the Negro, promoted to this position, acts only with reference to Negro employees. Many industries have had women personnel officials to act with reference to women. In one sense, this is an extension of the earlier and still existing practice of hiring from among a new ethnic group in industry a "straw boss" to look after them. The "straw boss" is the liaison officer reduced to lowest terms.

Another solution which also results in a kind of isolation if not in segregation, is that of putting the new people in the library or laboratory, where they get the prestige of research people but are out of the way of patients and the public. Recently, industries have hired a good many Negro chemists to work in their testing and research laboratories. The chemist has few contacts with the production organization. Promotion within the laboratory will put the Negro in charge of relatively few people, and those few will be of his own profession. Such positions do not ordinarily lead to the positions of corresponding importance in the production organization.

They offer a career line apart from the main streams of promotion to power and prestige.

These solutions reduce the force of status contradiction by keeping the new person apart from the most troublesome situations. One of the consequences is that it adds new stories to the superstructure of segregation. The Negro hospital and medical school are the formal side of this. The Negro personnel man and foreman show it within the structure of existing institutions. There are evidences that physicians of various ethnic groups are being drawn into a separate medical system of hospitals, clinics, and schools, partly because of the interest of the Roman Catholic church in developing separate institutions but also partly because of the factors here discussed. It is doubtful whether women will develop corresponding separate systems to any great extent. In all of these cases, it looks as if the highest point which a member of these odd groups may attain is determined largely by the number of people of his own group who are in a position to seek his services or in a position such that he may be assigned by other authority to act professionally with reference to them. On the other hand, the kind of segregation involved may lead professional people, or others advanced to special positions, to seek—as compensation—monopoly over such functions with reference to their own group.

Many questions are raised by the order of things here discussed. One is that of the place of these common solutions of status conflict in the evolution of the relations between the sexes, the races, and the ethnic groups of our society. In what circumstances can the person who is accepted formally into a new status, and then informally kept within the limits of the kind mentioned, step out of these limits and become simply a lawyer, foreman, or whatever? Under what circumstances, if ever, is the "hen doctor" simply a doctor? And who are the first to accept her as such—her colleagues or her patients? Will the growth of a separate superstructure over each of the segregated bottom groups of our society tend to perpetuate indefinitely the racial and ethnic division already existing, or will these superstructures lose their identity in the general organization of society? These are the larger questions.

The purpose of the paper, however, is not to answer these large questions. It is rather to call attention to this characteristic phenomenon of our heterogeneous and changing society and to suggest that it become part of the frame of reference of those who are observing special parts of the American social structure.

The Knitting of Racial Groups in Industry [12]

Elton Mayo has recently given the name "rabble hypothesis" [13] to the assumptions which, he claims, still guide not merely many managements in dealing with workers, but also many of those who investigate industrial behavior. He refers to the belief than an industrial organization is an aggregation of individuals each seeking his own gain without reference to other persons, and consequently each capable of being induced to greater effort by devices focused upon this desire for advantage. To this assumption Mayo opposes the view that a working force normally consists of social groups, whose members are highly responsive to each other's social gestures and identify their fates with those of their fellows; social groups which, further, are related to others in the larger system of social relations in and about industry. Mayo argues that a state of good cooperation is dependent upon the existence of such groups, even though one of their functions may

12. By Everett Cherrington Hughes. A paper presented before the American Sociological Society at the 40th Annual Meeting, March 1-3, 1946. Reprinted from *The American Sociological Review*, XI, no. 5 (October, 1946), pp. 512-9.

13. *The Social Problems of an Industrial Civilization*. Boston, 1945. Chapter II, and passim.

be some restriction of individual production. He believes, finally, that the "solitary," the person who does not feel himself part of any such group, is actually somewhat disorganized, and not likely to function well in the long run.

The theme of my remarks is that a fruitful way of analyzing race relations in industry is to look at them against whatever grid of informal social groupings and of relations within and between such groups exists in the industries, departments and jobs in which Negroes or other new kinds of employees are put to work. Recent experience suggests that this grid of relationships, and the manner in which Negroes are introduced into it, are more significant in the success of a policy of hiring Negroes than are the generalized racial attitudes of the white workers concerned.

Polling of white workers to find whether they favor the hiring of Negroes as their equal and close fellow-workers would almost anywhere result in an emphatic "No." Workers generally prefer not to have any new kinds of workers introduced among and equal to themselves. But Negroes have been successfully employed among white workers; and many other new kinds of workers have been introduced among older kinds of workers who were not enthusiastic about them. Polling of attitudes, on this simple basis, gives little clue to the probable behavior of the old workers to the new. The simple "No" of the workers to many proposals of management is not to be taken at face value; for industry has not been run by majority vote of the workers, and a "No" is often no more than a demonstration of protest. In fact, workers more or less expect each other to object to changes proposed by management.

It does not follow that racial preferences and dislikes have no bearing on the question whether the races will work well together. Racial attitudes themselves take on new dimensions when looked at in the framework of the human relations prevailing in industry. It is characteristic of industry that groups of workers who have knit themselves into some kind of organization in and about their work develop some set of expectations, considered little short of rights, that their jobs and their work-fellowship should be limited to persons of some certain kind—as to age, sex, race, ethnic qualities, education and social class. Mr. Orvis Collins, in a recent paper,[14] shows how the management of a New England factory got itself into an impasse by violating the expectation that certain kinds of jobs should belong to Irishmen. We could do with a good deal more investigation of what workers in various jobs and industries consider the proper kind of fellow-worker, what they think are their own rights in the matter, and of the devices which they use to expel newcomers not of the kind they want and of those which management and unions have used to get the newcomers accepted. Such expectations are not likely to be stated formally; they may not even be admitted informally. Defense of the breach of them is likely, as in the case reported by Mr. Collins, to be hidden by indirection of various kinds. It is also probable that some of the so-called non-economic behavior attributed to people new to industry—erratic changing of jobs, failure to respond to wage incentives, quitting industrial work entirely and returning home to farms—may be due not merely to unfamiliarity with the ways of industry. It may be a reaction to rejection by those among whom they have been put to work.

I used the expression "grid of informal relations." By this I mean simply the pattern of grouping which prevails in a place of work. The factory cafeteria, shown in Figure 1, exhibits such a grid; this is the pattern which renews itself every day at noon, when there are the most and the greatest variety of people there. The employees sort themselves according to their rank, sex, and race, and to their places in the office or out in the plant. The observers found also, that while it was seldom possible for all of the workers who belonged to a given close circle to come to the cafeteria and find places at the same table, they did—so far as possible—eat together.

The individual thus finds his table in a grid of rank, sex,

---

14. "Ethnic Behavior in Industry," *American Journal of Sociology*, LI (January, 1946), 293-298.

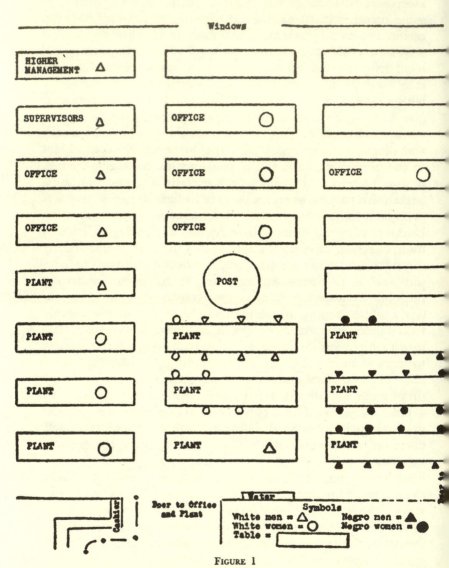

FIGURE 1

Seating by rank, sex and race in a factory cafeteria.

race, and personal relations. At a union picnic the unit of the pattern was the table, each serving as headquarters for one or two family parties. The management families were in one corner of the grounds; the mass of the Negro families were concentrated toward the opposite corner. In the middle zone were some tables at which a Negro family party and a white family party sat, but so grouped that Negro faced Negro and white faced white. Near the platform used for announcements, dancing and contests, were the only tables with racially mixed parties. These were the union leaders in charge of the picnic. Thus, in this grid, the family—which is by American definition not racially mixed—and rank within the factory worked together to form a pattern, which the union slightly disturbed by drawing a few people away from the family and away from factory rank to form a small nucleus based on special function.

I mention these examples first, not because of the inherent significance of seating arrangements in cafeterias and at picnics, but because they illustrate so vividly what I mean by a grid of relationships. Incidentally, in both cases the Negroes—with the exception of the few union committeemen at the picnic—fitted into that space in the pattern whose occupants were most numerous and of the lowest rank. None of them had characteristics which would set up any expectation that they might fit anywhere else.

On the job itself, the patterns of relationship are subject in varying measure to the physical lay-out of the shop, the distribution of workers of different races among the various kinds of jobs, by the degree of dependence of one worker upon others for successful performance of his work, as well as by the social atmosphere created by management, supervision, the union and the workers themselves. Furthermore, the informal relations among workers are not always so immediately visible as in the cafeteria and at the picnic. But generally such relations are there, although not all workers are part of any network of groups of people who cooperate in some special way to control what goes on with reference to work or other matters.

THE FIXING ROOM

A department called the Fixing Room in a certain plant illustrates one kind of grid or grouping at work and its consequences for race relations. The work is done by teams of

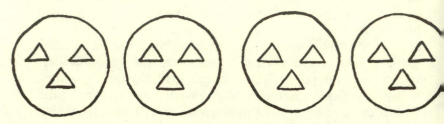

FIGURE 2. Fixing Room.
(Each circle is a closed work team of three men.)

three men. The members of a team meet and exchange tools and materials without a word and without even a direct look at each other. In fact, there is something of a cult of silence among them. The bonus, which is a large part of their income, is based upon the product of a team. The skills are learned on the job from the other members of the team to which one is assigned. The men are nearly all Poles, past middle age, bound together by kinship and neighborhood. The teams and the whole group together are notoriously and successfully impervious to management's attempts to control their relations, and even the choice of new employees. They pick their own fellows. The labor shortage of the war dried up the sources of new men of their kind and management tried to get new help—Negroes. Several Negro men were hired, but all left after a few days. Interviews with these Negro men revealed that they were subjected to a not very subtle, but very effective torture by the other members of the teams to which they were assigned. Later, the management tried the device of hiring a whole Negro team, which complicated the matter of learning the job; they stayed for some time, achieved a very creditable rate of production, and recently quit in a group. We have not yet found out what happened, but I venture to say that it was fundamentally a case of rejection by the older workers. In this shop there is no place for the solitary individual. One must be integrated into a team-clique to work at all. The homogeneity and traditional solidarity and autonomy of the whole department conspired to make the men unwilling to accept new kinds of workers and make management impotent to bring about change against their will.

The power of resistance was probably increased by connivance of the foremen. Many of the foremen in this plant are old-timers, who worked for the father of the present manager. They have a sort of proprietary interest in the departments they supervise; their idiosyncrasies are rather affectionately tolerated. The foremen can thus be, in effect, leaders of departmental cliques. A change of policy thus meets a very dense and intricate resisting structure. In their efforts to hire Negroes in the Fixing Room, management did not succeed in penetrating it.

THE POLISHING ROOM

The Polishing Room in another plant shows another type of both formal and informal organization operating in relation to race. In this room, each girl works independently on a machine like all the others. At intervals, all workers are moved along to the next machine. No one has a vested interest in a machine. By dint of good production and long service workers hope to get on the day shift. Many of the white girls of longer service have gravitated to this shift; it is about two-thirds white, in fact. The swing shift has a larger proportion of Negroes; the night shift, a strong majority of them. The few white girls on the night shift appear to prefer it because of some family reason. A girl cannot by especially high production increase her income; seniority alone brings small fixed increases of hourly wage; long service also brings certain benefits and an annual bonus. Something is made of the principle that only those who have good production records will be kept on when and if lay-offs become necessary.

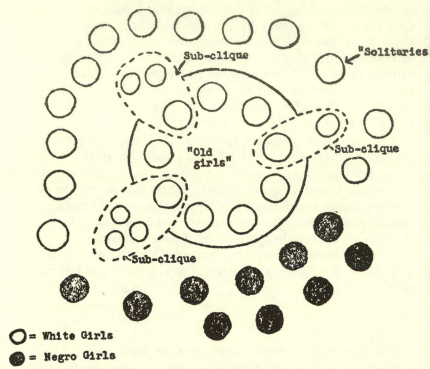

FIGURE 3. Polishing Room.

There is thus very little in the situation and in the policies of management to induce either a strong individualism or a close grouping of the employes. One would expect it to be a situation into which Negro help could be fairly easily introduced, and so it has been. But there is, nevertheless, an informal organization of workers. To quote from the report of the observers: [15]

"An analysis of clique formation and membership provides some clearer insights into such acceptance as the Negro has achieved and into the attitudes and expectation of Negro workers in the plant. There are several recognizable cliques in the Polish-

15. To preserve the anonymity of the plant, I must leave out the names of the observers. My apologies to them.

ing Room; their functions are well defined by their members. The clique is concerned with production and procedure, and with the status and behavior of the individual workers.

The cliques in this room are not mutually exclusive and sharply defined. There is a central group, the 'Old Girls,' made up of young women of from twenty-two to thirty-three years of age and of an average length of service of about five years. The 'Old Girls' eat in the cafeteria; each usually manages to eat with at least one or two of her clique fellows. Another group, also of long service, bring their lunches and eat in the lounge. But there is little association between them and the 'Old Girls' clique. There are a number of smaller satellite cliques, each attached by at least one common member to the 'Old Girls.' It appears likely that a new girl may be sponsored into the organization through the satellite cliques. We observed one girl who was, when first interviewed, unfriendly toward other workers, a 'lone wolf.' Two months later she had been accepted, had ceased to be a rate-busting 'horse' and had even become much more tolerant to the Negro girls."

The clique organization of the Polishing Room may be shown as in Figure 3.

The girls in the central clique, and those oriented towards them seem to be of such skill that they are without anxiety about being able to keep up to or even to surpass the usual rate; they maintain good levels of production, but make statements which make it clear that one of the functions of the group is control of the average rate of production.

White workers have defined a "good day's work" as falling within the limits of one hundred and one hundred and six. Many say that it would be easy to produce more. The girls who say this claim to be fast workers; they explain their failure to produce more by a well-developed rationale: to do more would be to ruin the job for the diligent, but slower workers. But "rate-breaking" is condoned for a day or so for a worker who has fallen behind and wants to bring her average up to par. Apparently a girl who is socially well established in the group can consistently break the rate a little with only mild teasing as punishment. But outsiders who break the rate are severely punished by ridicule and scorn; if they persist, they remain outsiders and, if associations are important to them, they may be forced off the job. Here is an apparent paradox: Admittance to the group may be secured only by adherence to the established definitions of the group, while unquestioned membership carries the privilege of some deviant behavior.

This is, of course, not a paradox at all; for it is characteristic of social groups to demand of the newcomer a strict conformity which will show that he accepts the authority of the group; then, as the individual approaches the center of the group and becomes an established member, they allow him a little more leeway.

Outside the organization are some white women and all the Negro women. The white women outsiders are a varied lot. Some are older women who must, or think they must, struggle to produce enough to keep their jobs. Some of them say that they are no longer young enough to be able to play. Others show in one way or another that some outside concern is so important as to make them defy or ignore the opinions of their fellow-workers. Some are probably not acceptable for one reason or another—perhaps dress, personal hygiene, or general queerness.

But no Negro girl, no matter what her length of service, her production rate, or her personality, has found a place in the system of cliques of the white girls. The observers report that among the girls in the cliques,

"It is generally understood that Negro workers are to be accorded tolerance and a measure of friendliness. There is ample evidence that there was opposition at first to the hiring of Negroes. In the two years that have elapsed a studied, but tentative acceptance has occurred. Negro and white workers meet each other with good will and friendliness on the job. They carry on conversations at their machines. But this friendliness does not extend beyond the work situation, and it varies in degree within the lesser cliques. White and Negro workers do not eat together except occasionally by accident. Not in any case is a Negro a member of a clique of white girls, and apparently conversation between the races seldom touches problems that are mutually important."

This means, in effect, that the Negro girls do not take part in the conversation of social gestures by which the rules and sentiments of the group are communicated to the newcomer, and by which she is offered membership in the clique as a reward for accepting its discipline. Insofar as white girls complain of the conduct of their Negro fellow-workers, it is in precisely the terms they use about white girls who are not in the cliques. The Negro girls, they say, "are all for themselves; they don't try to help each other." One white girl summed up the matter thus:

"Some colored girls . . . don't care what the next person does. They're that way about everything. If one of them makes a hundred and ten (a very high production), the rest of them don't care. Now when a white girl makes that much, we make her slow down because we know how hard it is for some of 'em to make the average."

Interviewer: "Why do you think the Negro girls don't try to pull their rates down?"

"Well, they're just like that about everything. They don't even try to help each other."

Interviewer: "What do you mean?"

"They don't get into a group. They just mingle with everybody. I don't think the colored girls have any little groups like we have. . . ."

Interviewer: "How do you account for that?"

"It's 'cause they're all for themselves. Now you take the white girls; the younger ones will mix with the older girls and they find out what they are supposed to do."

The same worker said of a new white girl "She won't keep no high average. She's mingling more with the other girls, now." Thus she implicitly recognized mingling with other girls and sensitivity to their opinions as a desirable, steadying experience. She apparently did not see that the very reason for the Negro girl's undesirable production habits is probably that she is excluded from the rewards of group membership. In effect, she is complaining that the Negro girls do not form their own cliques.

That the Negro girls have not developed an organization in this case is borne out by the observers. We do not know why this is so. But certain considerations concerning the probable reasons bear directly on the points thus far made and on the final one which I have to make.

Some of the white girls are, to use Mayo's expression, "solitaries." Most of the Negro girls are so. The records of production seem to indicate this, as well as their other actions and talk. A few Negro girls have very high rates, and indulge in racing with other workers. Some are erratic in production. Others anxiously struggle to get their rates up to the point where they can feel secure against being the first to be laid off. There is evidence that they think that they are on trial. This is highly individualistic behavior; is is also typically anxious behavior.

We may ask, although we cannot answer with much assurance, why the Negro girls in this room are so unorganized. First they are not in the white clique organization because they are not given the chance to be in it. Then, why do they not form an organization of their own? Perhaps because they are new, relatively speaking. Perhaps because on the day shift, where the main white clique developed, they—the Negro girls—are in the minority and would hesitate to form what would be considered a rival group. Perhaps it is that there are no Negro girls who feel secure enough in their positions to form a disciplining group which would, as part of its discipline, control production. In this particular plant the management has undoubtedly made a strong attempt to reduce discrimination. Now the way they have done it is to emphasize that the Negro girl will be hired, kept and promoted strictly according to her individual merits.

This is a point on which we may make some tentative generalizations. This very emphasis on treating the individual on his merits can become a source of over-individualistic anxiety. For the statement "You will be judged on your own merits," repeated too often becomes a dinning into one's ears of the thought, "You are on trial. I doubt whether you can make it, but if you do I will give you credit. Most people of your kind can't make it. I shall be astonished if you do. If you do, you will certainly be an exception. You've got to show me." This bit of imagined talk is, in fact, not far from what foremen do say to Negro workers in many plants. It contains an invitation, almost a threatening command, to the Negro worker to be a "solitary."

Now this might not work with Negroes of the least ambitious class or those working at traditional Negro jobs. But in the Polishing Room the Negro girls show potential or actual middle-class behavior and sentiments, as do also most of the white girls; nor are they employed at "Negro jobs." And this brings us to our general point. The individualistic or "rabble" hypothesis of industrial management—that each worker is an individual who may be induced, and who ought to be able to be induced to work for his own ends without regard to his fellows—is almost unconsciously applied with redoubled force to the Negro worker. The behavior it encourages is, in its essence, the behavior of the ambitious person. The ambitious white worker may dissociate himself from his fellows to some extent, and in spite of being somewhat disliked he may get promotions for it. The Negro worker apparently feels and is made to feel in some situations that he has to dissociate himself from others and be a "solitary" in order merely to keep his job. I do not think the Polishing Room is a situation in which this is unusually so. But the combination of individually separate work, with the particular pattern of white informal organization from which Negroes are excluded, and a management policy which gives the Negro girls definite hope that they can gain security by individual effort—and in no other way—might be expected to keep them a somewhat anxious series of solitaries rather than a stable organized group.

The Fixing Room illustrates the problem which arises in a shop where the informal organization consists of a series of closely related tight teams into which the individual worker —white or Negro—must fit in order to work at all. The

Polishing Room has an open formal structure, easy for the individual to enter; and a moderately open, but nevertheless, powerful, informal structure of cliques. But it is not quite open to Negroes, and the results are as have been reported.

These two cases are, however, alike in that no attempt has been made to modify the informal organization so as to relate Negroes to it. In the Fixing Room, after a first attempt to put Negroes into existing teams failed, management attempted to set up Negro teams, but without trying to define their relations to existing teams. In the Polishing Room, management tried to create general tolerance. In other cases, a union or management has made a more definite effort in this regard. It seems fairly common for a vigorous union administration successfully to encourage bi-racial groups of shop leaders. We have observed a few cases in which foremen who are the centers of informal groups of their own workers, have developed something of an inter-racial organization. More often the opposite occurs where the foreman occupies such a position. I cite these additional cases, without the description necessary for you to judge of them, to indicate the variety of situations which may occur, and also to introduce a final point; namely that the situation may often be changed by some active force, either union or management, which takes the pattern of informal relations into account.

Social Change and Status Protest:
An Essay on the Marginal Man [16]

The phrase "marginal man" and the phenomenon it designates came formally into the study of society with the publi-

---

16. By Everett Cherrington Hughes. Reprinted from *Phylon*, First Quarter, 1949, pp. 58-65.

cation of Robert E. Park's essay, "Human Migration and the Marginal Man" in 1928. I call it an essay, for it has depth, breadth and richness of hypotheses, neither required nor expected in an ordinary scientific paper. Park planted seed enough to keep a generation of scientific cultivators busy.

While the phrase came with this publication, the essential idea is much older. Park refers to many others who had sensed the problem; notably Simmel, in his passages on the "stranger" in his *Soziologie* and Gilbert Murray, in his *Rise of the Greek Epic*. He takes Heinrich Heine as a living example of the thing about which he is talking. What Park did was to put the "marginal man" into a broader setting; to see him as a function of the break-up and mixing of cultures attendant upon migration and the great cultural revolutions. He turned a literary and poetic insight into a cluster of related scientific hypotheses. In doing so, he brought it down from the glamour of antiquity and the grandly historical to the level of the most modest European immigrant as well as the oft despised mulatto and indeed even to all men in his remark that there are "periods of transition and crisis in the lives of most of us that are comparable with those which the immigrant experiences when he leaves home to seek his fortunes in a strange country."

The first part of Park's paper sketches broadly the relation of migration to cultures and social organization, leading up to its part in the break-up of the smaller traditional societies of which anthropologists have become the most expert students. The latter part focuses attention on the subjective aspects of migration and its effect upon human persons.

The first such effect he notes is "emancipation," the freeing of a man from customary expectations by travel and migration. Sometimes, we gather, the emancipated man is eager for new things; he explores and invents. In other cases, he may be painfully homesick for that which he left behind. Perhaps this homesickness is greatest when, as in the case of the Greek, that warm and sacred world for which he yearns no longer exists.

From the completely emancipated man, Park moves on to the "cultural hybrid:"

... a man living and sharing intimately in the cultural life and traditions of two distinct peoples; never quite willing to break, even if he were permitted to do so, with his past and his traditions, and not quite accepted, because of racial prejudice, in the new society in which he now sought to find a place.

The prototype of the "cultural hybrid" he found in the Jew emerging from the Ghetto. However, the person of mixed blood—to use the most misleading phrase of common talk about the races—is perhaps the most permanently and fatally condemned of all to the condition of marginality. And that fact, in so far as it is one, points to the true nature of the marginal position; for while the racial hybrid is ordinarily also a cultural hybrid, by virtue of the fact that both cultures and races develop their distinguishing marks in relative isolation, we have plenty of evidence in America that the racial hybrid need not be a cultural hybrid at all. The American Negro—whether of mixed blood or not—is not conspicuously a cultural hybrid. But he is a man with a status dilemma. And the more he, as an individual, acquires of those elements of American culture which bring to others the higher rewards of success, the greater is his dilemma.

In addition, the educated American Negro is a living contradiction of the canons of status in the American culture. The contradiction lies in the fact that a member of a group assigned a very humble and limited status bears other characteristics which ordinarily give or allow the individual to acquire higher status. The contradiction is objective, in that it appears to the eyes of others. The dilemma lies in the fact that he cannot accept the status to which Negroes are ordinarily assigned, but neither can he completely free himself from it. The dilemma, on the other hand, is essentially subjective. The Negro who passes as white no longer presents any contradiction to the eyes of others, but he still has the inner dilemma.

It is from the angle of status that I propose to analyze the phenomenon of marginality. Status is a term of society in that it refers specifically to a system of relations between people. But the definition of the status lies in a culture. In fact, one of the essential features of a person's status may be his identification with a culture.

Imagine a society in which the statuses are very well established. The rights and duties pertaining to each are well understood and generally beyond doubt and discussion. The ways by which an individual is assigned to and enters a given status are likewise well defined: by descent, sex, social learning and accomplishments of various kinds, arriving at a certain age, or by certain rites of passage, such as initiation and marriage. In such a case, one would expect—and the evidence on such societies seems to warrant it—that persons of a given status would exhibit a whole complex of social attributes, all of which seem naturally to pertain to that status. These attributes would be unconsciously woven into a seamless garment. Finally, everyone would know exactly who he is. His status identification would be clear and unquestioned by himself or others.

Imagine now the opposite—a society which is a complete free-for-all. Talents, both the virtuous and the nefarious, have full play. Everybody gets exactly what he has coming to him by virtue of his own efforts. It is a society without a hang-over from its past. If an enterprising lad of twenty were fittest to be head surgeon of a great hospital, he would be it. Make it more drastic; if a Jewish Negro girl of twenty, born in Russia and converted to the Witnesses of Jehovah were fittest to be head surgeon of Massachusetts General Hospital, she would be it. In such a society one could, in effect, say that status did not exist. Competition, of some purer sort than any we know, would determine without time-lag what each person would do and be. No such society ever existed. The ones we know are somewhere between this and the other pole. Relatively, our society is nearer the free-for-all than have been most others we know of.

Free as is competition in our society, and strong as is the strain toward allowing talent and accomplishment free rein, there are many positions about which there is a halo of technically irrelevant, but socially expected characteristics. Thus the physician is still rather expected by most people to be a man. He is expected, further, to be of a certain age, and, often, to have certain ethnic and class characteristics. But in our mobile and changing society new kinds of persons continually acquire the technically and formally demanded skills or qualities of a profession, or other position. Whenever it happens, sociological news is made and a new and unexpected combination of social characteristics appears; thus, the woman senator, the Negro judge, a boy president of a university, a professor in the White House, Cinderella in the Rockefeller mansion. For certain positions there is a long period of training for inculcating the auxiliary characteristics of a status as well as the technical skills. Thus, a medical course is a long *rite de passage*. So is the seminary of the priesthood and the novitiate of a religious order. Essentially, the function of the novitiate is to guarantee that there shall be no *marginal* priests or monks. The marks of the world are to be washed off, so that the new-born priest shall be fully a priest, acting as such and judged as such by all other priests and by all the faithful.

Now it is not merely that the new people who come into positions lack certain expected characteristics, but that they positively belong to groups which themselves have a status definition which includes a combination of expected characteristics. (Such combinations are called stereotypes.) The woman has certain traditional expected characteristics; she plays certain traditional roles. People are accustomed to act toward women in certain ways. Likewise, the Negro has a traditional role. The traditional roles of neither woman nor Negro include that of the physician. Hence, when either of them becomes a physician the question arises whether to treat her or him as physician or as woman or Negro. Likewise, on their part, there is the problem whether, in a given troublesome situation, to act completely as physician or in the other role. This is their dilemma. It arises from the fact that the culture has not yet provided a series of accepted definitions of behavior for the various situations which arise from the existence of this new kind of person. So long as the dilemma is present in the mind of the person, and so long as the existence of such a person appears a contradiction to others, just so long are the persons concerned in a marginal position.

Their marginality might presumably be reduced in several ways.

1. All such persons could give up the struggle, by retiring completely into the status with which they are most stubbornly identified by society. This people sometimes do. There are records of turning back to one's own people, culture or status which read like those of religious conversions, with conviction of sin, seeking and finding the light, doing penance and retiring into an exclusive world as into a cloistered religious order. Sometimes, however, such people become leaders of a cultural revival, which may be either religious or militant in temper.

People of the statuses threatened by marginal people generally favor this first solution—that of putting them back into their traditional places. Measures of repression and of exclusion are used to this end.

2. One of the statuses could disappear *as a status*. The word "woman" could cease to have social meaning, and become merely a biological designation without any status or role connotations. A few women have set this as the goal of the feminist movement. The word Negro would disappear—as it has tended to do in certain times and countries—in favor of a series of terms which would describe complexion and feature. These terms, in a continuum from black to white or white to black, would be of use mainly to people who are careful about the color of their dresses and neckties and to the police, whose vocabulary for identifying complexions of wanted persons has always been meagre. In short, there would be no Negro group to which to belong.

3. Persons of marginal position might individually resign from the status which interferes with their other status aims. A woman who became a physician would simply not be a

woman any more, although other people might remain identified with the status of women. A Negro would declare himself no longer a Negro. Such resignation is both subjectively
and objectively difficult. The interplay of these two aspects
of the difficulty constitutes a fascinating and sometimes tragic
theme of human drama. The temptation to resign, and even
to repudiate, is put heavily upon marginal people, as many
a Negro can testify. If a Negro worker is somewhat accepted
by white fellow workers in industry, they generally seem in-
wardly compelled to extract from him an admission that he
is an exception among Negroes. If he is like them in the rest,
why should he not be like them in their stereotypes also.
It is a kind of betrayal to which we are all subject in some
degree. When we yield, the cock crows thrice.

4. One or both of the statuses might, without disappearing, be so broadened and redefined as to reduce both the
inner dilemma and the outward contradiction.

5. Another possible solution is elaboration of the social
system to include a marginal group as an additional category
of persons with their own identity and defined position. A
number of people of similar marginal position may seek one
another's company, and collectively strive to get a place for
themselves. The Cape Coloured of South Africa, and the
Eurasians of India are groups of this kind. In this country,
the colored creoles of Louisiana, certain rural communities
of light-colored people in both South and North, and the
free Negroes in certain Southern communities in slavery
times all attempted with some success to establish themselves
as recognized groups, neither Negro nor white. During their
time of success, they were exclusive of other persons who
sought admittance to their ranks as every new member was
a potential threat to their special status. They became, in
fact, groups of kin-connected families; hence, something
closer to Indian castes than anything else in America has
been. But the strain toward keeping the American race system a simple dichotomy has worked against them. In recent
times, when nearly everyone must have "papers" for relief,

the draft, school, and the like, only the most "backwoodsy" of such groups can escape the fatal dichotomy.

The marginal groups just mentioned consist each of people who are marginal in the same way, and who consciously seek to fortify a common marginal position. Sometimes it happens that marginal people establish and live their lives in a marginal group, hardly knowing that they are doing so. There are whole segments of marginal society, with their marginal cultures among various ethnic and religious groups in this country, some of whom even developed a distinguishing speech. Large numbers of unmarried career women in American cities live in essential isolation from other women and with only formal contacts with men. In addition, there are other marginal groups who are not quite aware of their marginality, by virtue of living together a somewhat insulated life, but who are, furthermore, made up of people of the most diverse backgrounds; people who have in common, to start with, nothing but their marginality. These are to be found in cities and especially among young people. They are the American Bohemians.

All of these solutions appear as themes in the process of social and cultural adjustment and conflict. One can see in social movements—cultural, national, racial, feminist, class —all of these tendencies. The woman's movement has had its advocates of complete eradication of sex as a status determinant, its women who individually resigned from their sex and encouraged others to do so and those who have quietly or fervently gone back to and idealized the old roles. The main trend has been toward redefinition and broadening of the roles consonant with the status of women, and toward seeking also the integration of women into formerly exclusively male roles. One or another solution may be tried and given up. The internal politics of a social movement turns about choice of these solutions. If you will look inside any movement concerned with the status of a group of people and of their culture, you will find these conflicting tendencies. Shall it be a Negro Renaissance with return to Africa, individual "passing," a fight for disappearance of Negro as a status identifica-

tion, or some broadening and easing of the definition of the
Negro status? I need not remind you of the many contingencies in such choices. In reality, a given solution is seldom
adopted and stuck to to the exclusion of all others. There is
a sort of dialectic of them as the pursuit of one changes the
situation so as to bring another to the fore.

Up to this point, I have kept women and Negroes before
you as illustrations of people with a status dilemma. American Negroes, product of migration and of the mixing of races
and cultures that they are, are the kind of case to which the
term marginal man has been conventionally applied. I have
used the case of women to show that the phenomenon is not,
in essence, one of racial and cultural mixing. It is one that may
occur wherever there is sufficient social change going on to allow the emergence of people who are in a position of confusion of social identity, with its attendant conflicts of loyalty
and frustration of personal and group aspirations. Migration
and resulting cultural contact simply create the grand fields
on which the battle of status is fought out among humans; a
confusing and bloodier battle because its essence is that so
many people are in doubt about which side they want to be
on or may be allowed to be on.

In our own society the contact of cultures, races and religions, combines with social mobility to produce an extraor-
dinary number of people who are marginal in some degree,
who have some conflict of identity in their own minds, who
find some parts of the social world which they would like to
enter closed to them, or open only at the expense of some
treason to things and people they hold dear. American fiction has been full of such people, as it must be if it is to tell
the story of America. Even English fiction of the nineteenth
century abounds in such characters. Anthony Trollope's her-
oes and heroines are generally people who have more breeding than money, or more money than breeding. There are
young men who can go into politics and stay in high society
if they remain single or marry pots of money; but can be
true to a half-promise to some poorer, dearer girl only by
giving it all up and going to work for a living. Trollope's

own story, told in his autobiography, is that of a boy who went to Harrow school so shabby and penniless that he was the butt of cruel jokes from masters and fellow pupils for the twelve years he was there.

In Trollope's England, marginal social position was almost entirely a matter of class mobility. There was little of ethnic difference in it. In America, marginality is thought of as resulting solely from the mixtures of cultures, races and religions. There may be more of the problem of class mobility in it, however, than Americans have been accustomed to admit.

In mentioning what you may think the trivial case of Trollope's young man who must choose between his career (class position) and his sweetheart, I incidentally introduced a crucial problem of marginality to which there is little allusion in the formal discussion of the subject, that of life or career contingencies in relation to status marginality.

I suppose a person is furthest from a marginal position if he is so placed that he can go clear through his life without status dilemma. Each of us lives part of his life in retrospect, part in the fleeting present, part in prospect. We see ourselves in a running perspective of the human life cycle. Each phase of our lives offers its own status definitions, rewards and punishments; each phase also has meaning as the preparation for the next. In Jules Romains' *Men of Good Will* there is a conscientious little boy who promises himself the indulgence of leisure after completion of self-appointed tasks of study repeated so and so many times. The tasks get greater and greater and the indulgence gets put off further and further as he grows up. In the end he becomes very like a case reported by the psychoanalyst, Abraham; that of an artist* who promises himself a vacation as soon as he shall have produced a really worthy painting. He ends up, a sleepless wreck, in the hands of a psychiatrist. This is, in varying measure, the theme of life of all people who set high goals for themselves. It is the theme of balancing present and future.

Looking at this problem from the standpoint of social

organization, there are phases of life in which society is more open and more tolerant of diversity than others. Student life is traditionally such a phase. People of various races, ethnic groups, class backgrounds, and of the two sexes mix in an adventuresome spirit of Bohemianism. The essence of Bohemianism is disregard of convention. Convention, in its turn, is in large part a set of definitions of status, hence of proper behavior. Student Bohemianism is a conventional relaxation of convention.

Now university life is two things, a *rite de passage* and a preparation for careers. In England, the two things are crystallized in two kinds of degrees. The Pass degree is a *rite de passage* for sons of aristocrats and plutocrats; the Honors degree, which requires work, is for people who have to make their way in the world, as most American students must do. But university life is here also a *rite de passage*, not merely from the status of adolescent to that of adult, but from one way of life to another and, in many cases, from one culture or sub-culture to another.

The freedom of student life has always been tolerated by older adults on the assumption that it would, for each given individual, soon come to an end. We must then ask, both as social scientists and as persons with a life to lead, what are the hazards of passing from so free a phase of life into those which follow: of the transition from school to work, from irresponsible singleness to more or less responsible marriage, from young childless marriage to parenthood. Each of these has its hazards. Each of them generally brings one face to face with a stiffer set of status definitions, with greater mutual exclusiveness of social roles and consequently, with the greater possibility of status dilemma. This aspect of the problem of marginality has been very little studied. It is one of the crucial areas of study if we are really to advance our knowledge of modern society.

Before stopping, let us ask, with regard to social mobility and social change, the same question as we did earlier concerning the relation of migration to marginality. Are mobility and change necessary conditions of marginality, or are they, too, merely the favoring gale? Might there not be, in the most settled society, persons who are in protest against the roles assigned them; persons, even, who want to play some role for which there is no precedent or defined place in their culture? Need one have a woman's movement in order to have the individual woman who feels the masculine protest? Are all the inglorious village Miltons of unpoetic cultures so mute as those in Gray's Churchyard? I have often thought that the French-Canadian culture is so stable, not because of its isolation, but because there has been a whole continent for its free-thinkers and other rebels to escape into. I do not think we know the answer to these questions. But we have some clues. They suggest that the human individual does not always passively accept society's answer to the question, "Who am I?" with all its implications of present and future conduct. I suppose we might distinguish between that kind of protest which is merely a squirming within the harness, and that which is a questioning of the very terms and dimensions of the prevailing status definitions. At any rate, there is still much work to be done on the genesis of status protest; or, to put it the other way, on the processes by which the human biological individual is integrated—always in the presence and by the agency of other human beings—into a status system.

Index